W9-DCC-919

Praise for *The X-Economy*

Like the X on the treasure maps of old, Koulopoulos marks the intersection of commerce, connectivity, and community in the new X-Economy.

> *Don McLagan, retired founder, CEO and chairman NewsEdge*

The X-Economy is a thoughtful and challenging approach to the confused world of technology and business.

> *Jim Champy, chairman Perot Systems Consulting, co-author* Reengineering the Corporation

A well written, insightful book full of valuable information about the realities of the market place and the future of organizations by someone who deals daily with the staggering changes we all must face, whether prepared for them or not.

> *Dee Hock, founder and CEO Emeritus, VISA, author of* Birth of the Chaordic Age

At last, a book that grasps the fundamental concept that the Internet is more than just a way to squeeze a few margin points out of a business model, but will in fact drive fundamental changes in the way a corporation functions.

Tom Koulopoulos is the most significant visionary in high tech today because his observations and analyses are based upon solid research combined with the practical experience of helping hundreds of top executives make their organizations more productive.

> *Geoffrey James, author* Success Secrets of Silicon Valley, *radio talk show host, WRKO*

It is truly the first comprehensive look at how the new "X-economy" will change all the rules of commerce. It's the X-economy "business 101" for defining the new rules of engagement and providing managers to CEO's a thought provoking foundation for building a successful enterprise within the X-economy. Well done!

> *James K. Davidson, president and CEO, NTE (National Transportation Exchange)*

The first in-depth explanation of the new world of B2B e-commerce, and how the emerging phenomenon of Internet exchanges is changing the rules of business.

> *Lester Craft Jr., editor-in-chief,* eCommerce Business *magazine*

Koulopoulos and Palmer make a compelling argument that, to succeed in a world where technology overcomes the limitations of time and enables the customer to drive demand, business must encourage, not fear, the growth of vital, dynamic exchanges.

> *Shikhar Ghosh, founder, OPEN MARKET; founder, CEO and president, VERILYTICS*

Revealing, compelling and concerning. For anyone that thinks they can become comfortable with recent dot com demise, think again. Koulopoulos shows how the eXchange economy is here to stay, and that we all better learn how to deal with it. Whether we are victors or victims, this text demonstrates issues that will affect both the transaction and interaction of our future. A great read, this book will make us think hard before dismissing the Internet, and more importantly shows how we can leverage it.

Michael J. Cunningham, author of B2B *and* Partners.com

Koulopoulos has captured the essence of the new economy in a simple set of rules that applies to every business—new and old economy based—and every business leader.

Joseph Morone, president, Bentley College

A great book! Palmer and Koulopoulos offer crisp and timely examples that reveal the significance of the exchange paradigm. Together they construct a roadmap of the emergent forces that will guide businesses through this time of disruptive change.

Matthew Greeley, CEO and chairman, Brightidea, Inc.

A powerful, dynamic exploration of the key issues of the new millennium. The authors have written a superb book which provides a roadmap to help guide executives and managers in any company in any industry to better understand and address the major dynamics affecting future relationships, communities, markets, and market competition.

This book captures the essence and the spirit of what today's and tomorrow's leaders need to know and what they need to do to be successful in the new frontier. An absolute must read for every leader!

The Honorable Edward G. Lewis, former CIO and Assistant Secretary, US Government, president Enterprise Transpformation Group

Tom provides an exciting and thoughtful vision of the future. A must read for anyone who wants to understand the dynamic forces shaping the future of global business.

Patrick Smyth, vice president, Global Alliance Division, Compaq Computer Corp.

Business success hinges on building and leveraging relationships, which is at the core of the new economic communities this book explores. All members of these communities, from consumer to business leader, will find this book both illuminating and entertaining.

Ulf Arnetz, president and CEO, Corechange, Inc.

THE
X-ECONOMY

THE
X - ECONOMY

Profiting from Instant Commerce

Thomas Koulopoulos
Nathaniel Palmer

TEXERE

New York • London

CABRINI COLLEGE LIBRARY
610 King of Prussia Road
Radnor, PA 19087

HF
5548.32
.K68
2001

#46395295

Copyright © 2001 Thomas Koulopoulos and Nathaniel Palmer. All rights reserved.

Published by

TEXERE
55 East 52nd Street
New York, NY 10055

Tel: +1 (212) 317 5106
Fax: +1 (212) 317 5178
www.etexere.com

In the UK:

TEXERE Publishing Limited
71–77 Leadenhall Street
London EC3A 3DE

Tel: +44 (0)20 7204 3644
Fax: +44 (0)20 7208 6701
www.etexere.co.uk

Reproduction or translation of any part of this work beyond that permitted by Section 107
or 108 of the 1976 United States Copyright Act without the permission of the copyright
owner is unlawful. Requests for permission or further information should be addressed to
the Permissions Department, TEXERE LLC, 55 East 52nd Street, New York, NY 10055.
This publication is designed to provide accurate and authoritative information in regard to
the subject matter covered. It is sold with the understanding that the publisher is not
engaged in rendering legal, accounting, or other professional services. If legal advice or
other expert assistance is required, the services or a competent professional person should
be sought.

Library of Congress Cataloging-in-Publication Data has been applied for.

ISBN 1-58799-074-1

Printed in the United States of America

This book is printed on acid-free paper

10 9 8 7 6 5 4 3 2 1

To my Xrs
Mia, Adam, Michael, Sam, Olivia, Vernon, Corey, Andreas,
and those to come, that theirs may be an economy rich
in opportunity, spirit, and hope.

TK

To Heather,
whose love and support make it all possible and worth it.

NP

ACKNOWLEDGMENTS

The last task for any author is thanking those whose ideas, inspiration, and support make writing a book such as this possible in the first place. It is small recompense to find your name mentioned ever so briefly in these few words. But our gratitude and debt extends far beyond these pages.

This was a difficult book to write. Not so much because of the ideas, opinions, and research, challenging as these were, but due to the sea of change that is sweeping technical and economic landscapes.

It seems as though the hallmark of the new millennium is volatility in every aspect of life. While we were writing this book, the economic markets were in turmoil. Technology topics seemed to come and go like thunderbolts, each one illuminating the landscape for an instant followed by the din of media and then suddenly retreating into silence. Our own lives as authors, consultants, analysts, and educators seemed to be ever more fragmented with the luxury of focus a highly prized possession. Clearly, we were not alone. The world may be changing faster than it ever has, but we humans still have limits.

All of this is to say that the time each of the individuals here mentioned spent helping us to write this book is more valuable than ever—from the quality time that was otherwise owed to family and friends, which they donated to our efforts, to the time offered by associates and coworkers from already too-busy schedules. We thank:

The *long-time* members of the Delphi team whose insights, analysis, and camaraderie give us the support to do our work and the context to take pride in it. Carl, Nick, Debbie, Carlene, MaryAnn, Dan,

Linda, John, Jacqueline, Andrea, Debby, Tom, Stacie, Mark, Pasquale, Rich, Margie, Patrick, Larry, Ralph, Susy; our mates from down under, Jeff and Cedric; to the north, John Kunar; and to the east Hiroshi and Hiroyuki.

Special thanks to: Hadley for his work on the early versions of the portal material that became such a core part of the book; Jack for jumping in to offer feedback and crystallizing some of the early thinking around the structure of the book; and to Rob and Dan for their usual masterful job with the X-economy Website.

Our development editor, Corinne Gregory, for her help in working out the many kinks in the rough manuscript and coming up with the idea to include the "take aways" at the end of each chapter. Her perseverance and commitment to the book provided the much-needed bandwidth and objective critique necessary to get the project into high gear.

Our reviewers, who offered their kind words, comments, and praise: Jim Champy, Dee Hock, Don McLagan, Geoffrey James, Lester Craft Jr., Shikhar Ghosh, Michael J. Cunningham, Joseph Morone, Matthew Greeley, The Honorable Edward G. Lewis, Patrick Smyth, Ulf Arnetz, Richard C. O'Sullivan, and Jim Davidson.

George Simpson, who at a moment's notice did a photo shoot for us of Ephesus. His keen eye and superb photography brought me back to what is one of the most inspiring places on earth. We only wish that we could have included all 33 of his photographs in the book.

Jeanne Gorman who keeps life sane, often at the expense of her own sanity.

My greatest literary ally, John Willig, agent and friend through more book proposals and projects than I ever thought possible in one's lifetime, much less in such a short part of one's lifetime.

The entire team of Texere, especially Jena, Renea, Lia, Crickett, and Myles for their courage in breaking new ground in an industry that has for too long rested on sacred turf.

Brenda Hunter and the folks at Publications Development Company in Texas who were actually able to make sense of the seemingly endless stream of edits, scrawls, and last minute alterations.

Foxy Woodside, whose memory is never far from my heart.

Mike and Maria Koulopoulos for the courage, zeal, and curiosity they inspired in a young boy to challenge the world until it revealed its secrets.

Finally and most sincerely, we thank our families for their enduring support, patience, and praise. To be the wife, husband, son, or daughter of an author is to be an author—without choice. Debbie, Heather, Mia, and Adam, for the time we have taken and the time you have given, this is your book as much as it is ours.

TK
Boston
March 2001

CONTENTS

CHAPTER 6
Rule 5: The X-Economy Is Instantaneous, Get Used to It   193

PROLOGUE

Η δ αρχι λεγετε ημισυ ειναι παντος
The beginning is half the whole
Aristotle

Think of your last great idea. The product or service that was sure to revolutionize the world and make you or your company millions. What stopped you from making it a reality? Capital? Time? Let's say you had plenty of both. What obstacles would remain? Or, if your idea is now a global phenomenon, why did it succeed?

As an entrepreneur, business manager, or Fortune 100 CEO, the greatest challenge for all good ideas is identifying, establishing, and coordinating the network of suppliers, partners, and delivery channels required to get from concept to cash.

Building these intricate networks for producing and delivering goods—called a *supply chain*—is not trivial. Successful companies are those who have created an army of supply chains and who can effectively rebuild them for new innovations.

But building or rebuilding a supply chain assumes that the community of competent suppliers is known. In today's global markets, this is unlikley. The volume of innovation and the volatility of markets in the twenty-first century virtually assures that we will not know who the best prepared, most competent, and least costly supplier is for any specific task at any given time. Even when we know who the possible suppliers are and have established confidence in their ability to deliver on their products or services, there is the lengthy process of comparing and negotiating pricing, issuing requests for proposals and comparing quotations.

What if there was a way to do this instantly; to exhaustively identify partners, suppliers, and buyers; coordinate and rebuild intricate value chains (the collection of businesses, resources, and tasks that go into producing and delivering any product or service); respond to market needs that consumers cannot yet even express? What might that mean to innovation, competition, quality consumer options, the free market?

The new exchange economy—the *X-economy*—is the environment in which this kind of instant innovation can occur. The Internet is the tool for such change, providing the opportunity for unprecedented flexibility, collaboration, and speed. This is the commerce of the future.

Why an X-economy? *X* has a multitude of connotations. It is the symbol for a new generation, the unknown variable of an equation, the restricted territory outside of the social norm; in short, *X* is the terra incognito that lies forever just outside of our grasp.

First and foremost, the *X* is about the online exchanges that will rule our markets and our economies. These are the global exchanges where communities of trade will form and through which virtually all commerce will flow. Most of the focus of this book is on how these online exchanges will shorten the time it takes to form supply chains, partnerships, and products.

The *X* refers to the unknown variable that is now systemic to our economic models. Economies have always been unpredictable, but they had durations of certainty. Like weather patterns, economies moved in large slow arcs. Today, that luxury is lost. Markets, economies, and value chains move as microclimates—constantly volatile, constantly changing. There is no safe haven, no escape from the deluge of information on which to make economic decisions, no refuge in the maelstrom of alternatives, partnerships, and opportunities. This book considers ways to manage this uncertainty, and what has since become a global attention deficit disorder, through mechanisms that infuse markets with the ability to engender trust, create time, and ultimately establish new forms of community.

X represents the extremities of markets and the economy to which power has been slowly but surely shifting for centuries. Every social, political, and economic system is being further decentralized into entities that are apparently uncontrolled by centralized authorities and instead ruled by their communities.

Finally, the X represents the unlimited potential of an economy to flourish when it creates the mechanisms to extend prosperity to a global community. We explore the impact that this new *liquidity* will have on the economic prosperity of the enterprise and the individual.

What is most important to understand is that the X-economy is more than just networking an industry so that information can be shared electronically. There is certainly challenge in creating an instant enterprise by piecing together all of the requirements, schedules, availability, pricing, logistical, and contractual issues that each partner in the value chain may have to contend with. But there is much more.

The X-economy is a molecular economy of infinitely malleable and instantly responsive enterprises. This ability to rapidly form and reform the bonds that tie businesses together is not unlike the analogy of relationships among the basic process of any chemical interaction.

Consider, for example, the basic mechanics of water molecules, which consist of two hydrogen atoms and one oxygen atom bound together (hence the designation H_2O). Water molecules continually form bonds with other water molecules and also continually break these bonds, creating a constantly dynamic environment that is the basis for the fluidity of water.

Even more interesting, in the context of our X-economy analogy, is the recombinant characteristic of molecular models. By merely adding one new component—in this case, an atom—to an existing molecule, a completely new element can be formed. Our water molecule, H_2O, is a relatively inert element that is essential to every plant and animal on this planet. Yet, add only one simple oxygen atom, and suddenly we have a new substance, H_2O_2, or hydrogen peroxide, which is a far less stable compound.

Think of how water molecules form bonds that break rapidly when in a liquid state; whereas frozen water molecules form bonds that do not break easily. In their liquid state, the components of an economy instantly take the form of their markets. The result is near-zero lag time in every aspect of how markets behave.

In short, if you have a good idea at midnight, you may very well have a value chain constructed by 8:00 the next morning. This is a radical thought in itself, especially for those who are already succumbing to a market whose pace has far exceeded their tolerance for speed.

And it is just the beginning.

If Covisint (one of the benchmark exchanges we will discuss) lives up to its promise, consumers will be custom manufacturing their own automobiles at some point in the not too distant future. And their cars will be available the next day. Doug Grimm, director of global strategic sourcing for engine and chassis supplier Dana Corp., a Covisint exchange member puts it bluntly, "GM says that when somebody in a dealership orders a car with leather seats, the cow should wince." This is just a glimpse of what's to come.

Clearly we live in an era of upheaval in the social, political, and industrial fabric of our lives—an era that offers undreamed of opportunity to build a new framework for the future. But builders we all are not.

England's early nineteenth-century Luddites[1] took sledgehammers to the promise of the future. And many others followed. Their beef was not with the technology but with the purpose for which it was intended—to replace people. Yet if the nature of technology to change our lives and our work has taught us anything, it is that its progress deepens and focuses our own understanding, as a species, of our own core strengths and weaknesses.

So, what is the nature of the X-economy, and why should we not raise a Luddite fist against it? In short, what will it do for you?

The core strength and weakness of humanity is one and the same, *community*. We build elaborate forms of community with interactions prescribed in myriad ways through culture, society, legislation, and most often, commerce. The history of mankind is a history of evolving community, larger communities, and more sophisticated communities. Yet it is also a history of divided communities, intolerant communities, isolated communities, and, of course, competitive communities. We

---

[1] The Luddites were a band of textile factory workers led by a mythical Ned Ludd. Inspired by writers of the day, such as Thomas Paine, they opposed the use of automation in factories and protested by demanding higher compensation and better work conditions. Since then the label Luddite has been used to describe anyone opposed to technological progress.

Technology has always shaped—and driven—community, commerce, and connectivity. The X-economy is simply where all three converge.

believe strongly that connecting communities across the geographical, industrial, cultural, and economic divides that have come to typify economic man is the greatest challenge and greatest promise of online exchanges. Creating paths of interaction between communities of trade is the modern equivalent of establishing the trade routes for commerce in the pre-industrial world.

Focusing on how the evolution of commerce is going to shape this future may seem trivial when compared to the great debates surrounding world peace, global warming, and the ever-increasing divide between prosperity and poverty. Yet the paradigms that drive commerce provide the framework for most of the global consequences on which we must decide.

Global paradigms are the images of humanity's common memory. They provide an alignment and a context for our actions—the image of the earth floating in the blackness of space, which lead to the ecological movement—they are simple and singular, yet powerful and pervasive rallying points. Although, individually we can ascribe many emotions and meanings to these images, collectively we find a comon meaning for them—obscure at first, but in retrospect easily identified as a turning point.

The X-economy is such a milestone. It affords us the rare opportunity to revisit some of the most basic precepts in the way we connect our enterprises and ourselves; the principles we use to understand and react to the world of commerce; and the way we form communities of trade.

Creating paths of interaction between communities of trade is the modern equivalent of establishing the trade routes for commerce in the pre-industrial world.

Why be surprised? Technology has always shaped—and driven—community, commerce, and connectivity. The X-economy is simply where all three converge.

ABOUT THIS BOOK

In preparation for this book we conducted a study of 600 Fortune 1000 organizations. One of the most striking findings of this study was that 34 percent of the transactions in responding companies were already being conducted through electronic trading networks. Let's be clear. This is not e-commerce, dot-coms, or the consumer side of selling over the Internet. These are trading networks already established between business partners—they reflect the business-to-business transactions that are the backbone of a new exchange economy—the X-economy.

What is even more amazing is that the rate of increase in the number of these transactions has exceeded 30 percent yearly for the past three years. At this rate, nearly all business transactions will take place in some form of exchange in four to five years. That's how much time we have to put the ground rules we describe in this book in place and make them part of our organizations' everyday practices, attitudes, and cultures.

All this would sound like so much dogma if it weren't for the ground-level mechanics being put in place to make it practical reality. Understanding these mechanisms and all of the specific forces shaping the new exchange economy and then describing them in a book can be a significant challenge—for us and for you. This is why we narrowed down what you need to know to take action into five ground rules of the X-economy.

Each of the central chapters of this book discusses one of these five rules:

1. *The X-economy is driven by the demand chain not the supply chain.* Supply chains work by anticipating and predicting the needs and requirements of a market. Over time, however, supply chains become armies of procedure and policy, yielding

slowly to new requirements. Demand chains can now instantly express requirements through exchanges, which result in the formation of nearly instant product or service for new markets.

2. *The X-economy is a community not a market.* Markets behave in predictable fashion. Markets have trends and patterns. Markets will yield their preferences and habits to astute inquirers. However, communities defy rational analysis. They behave in ways that often surprise and confound. While markets consist of rational people who can be satisfied, communities consist of swarms that are never content. As instant communication accelerates, time-to-community economies are moving toward more chaotic states.

3. *The X-economy is built on trust not transactions.* Despite monumental investment in technology to build exchanges and online commerce, the greatest limiting factor in building the X-economy is trust and culture. If exchanges are to replace much less outpace today's methods of doing business, they must provide a trusted community.

4. *The X-economy is personalized.* The volume and velocity of information, partners, suppliers, and buyers in today's markets is far greater than could be effectively understood or managed through the computer desktop interfaces that we presently use. Creating a personalized "My" view of the world will be essential for the survival of the next generation of knowledge workers for whom attention will be the most hotly contested frontier.

5. *The X-economy is instantaneous.* The luxury of focus, idle time, stability, and analysis is all but gone. Time is a priceless and rare element. Businesses will measure their competitive advantage by how well they create time. Our ability to form connections faster has allowed organizations to disintegrate into much broader and more complex value chains. Exchanges have formed as a direct response to this situation and the resulting overnight disappearance of the latency in market interactions has vanished in step with the accelerated pace of life. With little or no lag time in transactions, both buyers and sellers have become ever more conscious of time as the key metric of success.

These ground rules were the result of studying 600 companies in various stages of transforming their business. Their experiences, attitudes, and competitive strategies point the way to entirely new models for business. Understanding these ground rules will not stem the tide of change, but they may help us to surf it.

This book is organized simply. Here is a suggested way to go about reading it.

The first chapter offers an introduction to the main concepts and tenets of the X-economy. Whatever else you do, read this chapter *first*.

The five main chapters that describe the rules may be read in any order. Each provides a separate perspective of the factors that are influencing and defining the formation of new exchanges.

Chapter 3 is the most technically oriented discussion in the book. Here we discuss the first examples of exchanges and the many business models of an exchange. You may want to skim this briefly and then come back to it if you are less interested in the technology, case studies, and mechanics of exchanges.

The epilogue offers a glimpse of the future from the same vantage point we start our discussion—community, but with a distinctly more personal flavor.

Last, and perhaps most important, the accompanying Web site (www.thexeconomy.com) gives you a chance to interact with us, the authors, and with other readers.

One final piece of advice before you begin: The temptation is always strongest to focus too tightly on how the rules we are describing may enhance current business, market, and work models rather than to stretch our imagination beyond the envelope of our experience.

The plethora of concepts and buzzwords bantered about during the advent of the Internet has jaded even the most optimistic among us. So it is no surprise then when confronted with the idea of the new exchange economy our first instinct is to wonder if it isn't just the same old economy on computers?

At first it is. The bastion of brick-and-mortar business that make up the old economy will not give ground easily. But you would be hard pressed to find a single old economy company that is unconcerned about its ability to maintain brand, supplier, and employee loyalty in the coming years.

Not long ago we at Delphi were visited by a company whose name is probably unfamiliar to most readers: Wienerberger. Although not a household name, Wienerberger is one of the world's largest manufacturers of bricks—the quintessential brick-and-mortar company. Their concern was simple, "How do we protect ourselves and our distributors from the disintermediating effects of a brick exchange?" It's the same question every old economy company is asking. No industry is exempt, from those who build with bricks to those who build with bits.

> Imagine yourself going back in time and trying to explain the concept of jet lag to a citizen of the nineteenth-century.

Our response was blunt and simple. The only decision Wienerberger has to make is, "Whose exchange will I be part of?" rather than, "Will I be part of an exchange?" Stalling this decision by focusing on how to deal with what we see as the inevitability of the exchange economy is tantamount to an early twentieth-century buggy whip manufacturer trying to convince themselves that a better buggy whip would stem the demand for automobiles.

The tide has turned. Swimming against it will only increase the distance we need to travel later to catch up.

But this does not mean a swift and sure journey awaits every entrant into the age of online, instantaneous exchange. The X-economy radically changes the rules of business and introduces new challenges as well as new opportunities. These concepts are so all encompassing and revolutionary it is nearly impossible for us to fully comprehend them.

Consider an analogy that is likely to be familiar to many: One of us just completed back-to-back flights to Europe and Australia from the United States, conducting business across twelve time zones in two weeks. At the end of it, flush with new opportunities but reeling from jet lag, it occurred to this weary author that there was a time when travelers did not have to worry about changing time zones—a time when their bodies had the chance to adjust slowly to the changes of their circadian rhythm. It was a time when the idea of "lag" was not even a conceivable state of being for travelers.

Imagine yourself going back in time and trying to explain the concept of jet lag to a citizen of the nineteenth-century, or for that matter the early twentieth-century. They would have no framework for understanding what it meant to move at a rate of speed that could get you to your destination before you had even left. Think of the first time you tried to comprehend the concept of crossing the international dateline and gaining or losing a day in the process!

In the same way that modern airplanes changed the very notion of travel, the X-economy changes the very nature of business by not only collapsing time, but also permitting us to realize complexities and opportunities that once were unimaginable.

Open your mind and the possibilities begin.

THE
X-ECONOMY

CHAPTER 1

The X-Economy

Sir, it is not a revolt, it is a revolution.

Duc DE Rochefoucald-Liancourt, to Louis XVI, King of France on the evening of 14th July 1789 after the fall of the Bastille.

The X-economy (*shorthand for the exchange economy*): A demand-driven network of real-time global exchanges that instantly brings together all of the resources needed to form a value chain.

Time-to-Community

On the Mediterranean coast of Turkey, some 500 kilometers from Ankara, lies the ancient city of Ephesus. Built in 1000 BC, Ephesus is now one of the most extraordinary excavations of ancient civilization. Its mosaic-lined streets, 25,000-person stadium and grand city plan are a magnificent testimonial to the art and science of ancient civilization.

As visitors walk down the main boulevard of Ephesus, they encounter what is perhaps the most impressive sight in the city, the striking three-story library of Celsus. The library towers over the city center, a reminder that the inhabitants of this metropolis were as hungry and as protective of knowledge as any netizin[1] of today's wired world. Ephesus forces us to ask how we, today, are any different. We are left fumbling for an answer.

As it turns out, the greatest testimonial to the striking similarities between the citizens of Ephesus and those of the twenty-first century lies in a ruin directly across the street from the library in a much less obvious setting.

What remains of this structure resembles the base of an old temple. As your tour guide sits you down on the odd foundation and recounts a typical day in the life of its inhabitants, you cannot help but wonder where you are sitting, what this must have been here at the epicenter of the city. Perhaps it was the old town hall, a meeting place, or the center of political and economic debate. Clearly, it has to have been important or it would not have merited such a prime location.

> Time-to-community has been steadily decreasing throughout civilized history, often with extraordinary implications.

Then as the discussion turns to the topic of plumbing and running water, it dawns on you that this "temple" is nothing other than the communal toilet. You chuckle at the thought of it. A monumental architectural blunder you suppose, realizing that the toilet was in the center of it all. The images any creative mind now conjures need no more elaboration in our description here.

There is some comfort in knowing that we have indeed advanced so far culturally. But the smugness of cultural and technological elitism

---

[1] Popular term for citizen of the Internet.

quickly fades when you realize that this is no miscalculation of the city planners. It is not a testament to a crude and primitive social order.

These were architects of great forethought. It was not by happenstance that the toilet was in the middle of the city.

Its objective and purpose is striking because of its sheer simplicity. It was here, in the middle of the city, that you were guaranteed a daily audience for the community—yes, using the toilet! And building a community was clearly a prime directive of the city's architects.

During the time of Ephesus, community was no less important than it is today, only the mechanisms differed. The idea of the exchange and the chaotic community it entails, which we so often associate with the Turkish Bazaar, is not madness but a directed effort to build efficiency into the socioeconomic fabric of a civilization.

Citizens of the great city of Ephesus were part of an extraordinary community. Figure 1.1 is the library of Celsus which housed thousands of ancient written works and the stadium which seated 25,000 people. Positioning the public toilets directly across from the library, in such a prominent part of the city, is a testimonial to how important community was to this civilization.

What has changed radically from the days of Ephesus to the exchanges of the X-economy is the most basic equation upon which our society is built—time-to-community. Time-to-community is the time required to build a community of similar social and/or commercial interests, and it has been steadily decreasing throughout civilized history, often with extraordinary implications. Take for example the impact that technologies such as the printed book, radio, telephone, television, cable, and the World Wide Web have had on our ability to form communities of interest. Each provides a venue through which to disseminate the rallying point for a community. And each of these has been able to reach increasingly larger constituencies in shorter time frames.

The number of years it took for each of these successive technologies to reach a population of 50 million has been dropping precipitously. The printing press took 100 years, the telephone took 25 years, and the

(a)

(b)

(c)

Figure 1.1   The architects of Ephesus placed community at the center of the city with the great library of Celsus (a) and the 25,000-seat amphitheater (b). However, even more startling is the public latrine located only a few steps from the library in the city center. If you look closely you can see clearly the individual facilities located along the perimeter of what, at first, seems to be a large temple (c). Although we may consider it crude, the conclusion is undeniable; it appears that little has changed in three thousand years when it comes to the importance of community other than the time to community.

World Wide Web took only 5 years. However, it's not just the scale and speed of community that has changed, but also the way in which we form community.[2]

Fast forward from Ephesus to the present day. As this book is being written, the first U.S. president of the twenty-first century is being elected. Fuzzy math, lock-box social security, and the many proposed applications of the national budget surplus will all have been duly recorded for posterity. The leader of the free world will be ready to take America forward into the new millennium.

But what will not go down in the history books is an event that may be far more significant—one that crystallizes the new paradigm of community for the twenty-first century. Barely newsworthy, it received little attention when it occurred during both the 2000 Democratic and Republican national conventions.

As is often the case at political rallies, protesters gathered in large numbers at both events, as did small armadas of police. But for the first time a phenomenon of extraordinary relevance was recorded at these protests.

Swarms of protesters armed with a new technology where able to evade police despite well-coordinated efforts by officials through land and air surveillance to thwart protesters and disband them.

Using cellular phones, protesters could broadcast their locations and tactics to fellow demonstrators in real time. As police attempted to block one path of entry or egress, the crowd would notify some other part of its community to relocate and take another avenue.

Organizing themselves as a swarm of insects with no leaders or singular points of failure the protesters evaded police continuously; no matter how many were arrested. So successful were the protesters and so frustrated were officials that police finally started arresting anyone with a cell phone under the charge of possessing an "instrument of crime."

This sort of "viral communication" is an undercurrent changing not only our notion of community, but also the most basic aspects of how we build a business and more importantly, how we lead it.

---

[2] This trend is actually an illusion of progress as we point out in the Epilogue.

Headless Leadership

Yet most value chains, as do most organizations, still cling to a command-and-control model that routes decisions through a central brain or "head."

Think of our protesters, a flock of birds, an ant farm, or even a colony of bees. The organizing principle in these groups is not the leader or the head but rather a series of decentralized decisions that act off of a common and shared set of rules or knowledge base.

The annihilation of buffaloes from the North American plain was in no small part due to the fact that a buffalo herd would freeze in its tracks when its leader was killed—making them a shooting gallery for hunters.

The misconception, like that of most theories of organizational learning, calls for people to cluster around an organizational leader like moths around a central flame. Although there are species that clearly play a simple game of follow the leader, these are often destructive behaviors in the face of drastic change. The North American Buffalo is a prime example.

The same principle has applied to militaristic institutions, many governments, and certainly traditional organizations. As Vincent Barabba, general manager of corporate strategy and knowledge development at GM, says, "The extent to which command and control is concentrated increases the vulnerability of the entire organization and, thereby the imperative to protect it—or, in the case of an enemy, to destroy it or cut it off from its fighting and supporting forces."[3]

Perhaps the quintessential case study of a decephalized enterprise is that of Visa International, the world's largest credit card processing organization with more than $1.75 trillion worth of sales.

Visa International was born out of the credit card-issuing orgy of the 1970s, when banks were so eager to grab market share that they were issuing pre-approved cards to anyone who could sign their name—and

---

[3] Vincent P. Barabba, *Meeting of the Minds: Creating the Market-Based Enterprise.* Harvard Business School Press, Boston, MA. 1995, p. 24.

hemorrhaging red ink in the process. In desperation, member banks appointed Dee Hock chairman of the newly formed TransAmericard Inc. (later Visa International), hoping that he would be able to impose discipline that the company needed. But Hock had something different in mind.

Instead of a public or private corporation owned by stockholders, ownership took the form of nontransferable rights of participation by member financial institutions. Even more unusual, these member companies were fierce competitors in the card-issuing market. Nevertheless, these companies needed to coordinate on several key issues, such as setting standards, managing a common clearing house, and supporting a common branding platform.

> The communities upon which we build today's commerce and enterprise rise and fall within minutes—consumer buying coalitions, business partnerships, networks of suppliers, distribution systems are formed in less time than an Ephesian could part a toga.

Hock realized this inherent conflict, but instead of enforcing cooperation by restricting what members could do, he encouraged the companies to compete and innovate. Visa card issuers are free to issue, price, and service products completely autonomously. As a result of the diversity of approaches, best-of-breed products and processes are far more likely to emerge. That stimulates the entire industry. Hock says, "At the same time, in a narrow band of activity essential to the success of the whole, they engage in the most intense cooperation." This apparent conflict of competition and collaboration has enabled Visa to adapt to new markets, currencies, competitors, products, and consumers' needs.

Hock deliberately designed the organization to decentralize intelligence into autonomous units as far as possible. Yet the organization's strategy and cooperation are more coordinated than many centralized organizations. Visa has been called "a corporation whose product is coordination," and "the only company in the world owned by its franchisees." Hock calls it an "enabling organization." He attributes its success to the combination of free-market enterprise and multiparty democracy the organization embraces.

In many ways, Dee Hock established the role model for the X-economy. In the X-economy, organizations rally around a community, rather than cluster beneath the oligopolists at the end of the value chain—and in the process remain true to their own needs and principles. The organizational structure, technology, and philosophy of enterprises that use a flexible framework allows them to adapt constantly and swiftly to environmental changes. As a result, these companies are always prepared to take advantage of market opportunities.

It may be a good idea here to stop and define community since we are using the term so liberally through out this book. Communities are collections of people governed by a common set of norms, conventions, and interests. Clearly, communities have many points of intersection and interaction with other communities. Even closed communities, such as the Pennsylvania Amish, who eschew modern means of production and transportation, still conduct trade with BMW driving atheists (not that the latter is necessarily a community of itself).

One of the key elements of any community is the ability of the community to take shape over time by aligning the otherwise selfish interest of its members into a single common good. This often takes time but once it's accomplished, communities are very difficult to break apart. The benefit to the individual is far greater in being part of the community than in striking out on their own or attempting to build a new community. This is in no small part the pathology of even the most destructive form of communities, cults.

Now consider, for a moment, what has changed about communities with the Internet. By creating a massive cauldron of individual interests that can be quickly matched, aligned, and coordinated the Internet has provided one of the richest fields for community to take root. And at a speed that not only allows much faster creation of a community but also allows individuals to participate in many more simultaneous communities. It is this last point that is most striking. By spreading the support systems across multiple communities, we significantly alter the velocity at which we move in and out of communities. The same principles apply to communities built for the explicit purpose of conducting commerce.

The communities upon which we build today's commerce and enterprise rise and fall within minutes—consumer buying coalitions, business partnerships, networks of suppliers, distribution systems are formed in less time than an Ephesian could part a toga.

Although the volume of opportunities is increasing rapidly, each opportunity is accompanied by increasingly shorter windows within which to make decisions (Figure 1.2). It is a phenomenon that permeates every aspect of community, and one that we will discuss throughout the book.

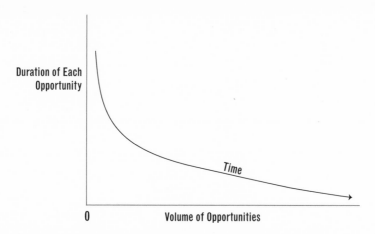

... the volume of telephone calls has increased by 300 percent while the average length of each call has dropped by nearly 30 percent.

Figure 1.2   The inverse relationship between opportunity volume and its duration. As volatility increases and all aspects of our lives accelerate, we have a perception that, despite an unprecedented abundance of opportunity, we have less time to take advantage and benefit from any single opportunity.

Based on data from the FCC, over the past two decades, use of the telephone has increased nearly ten-fold, while simultaneously, the intervals of use (e.g., the length of phone calls) have shrunk precipitously by nearly 30 percent! (See Figure 1.3.) Are the telephone and telephone calls appropriate proxies for how we form community? It seems that it is simply impossible for us to make any decision without an extraordinarily intricate network (read: community) of resources.

It all points to what is an inescapable conclusion; community is changing, spreading, and becoming the pervasive metaphor for commerce, enterprise, and technology. Leadership was a luxury. Despotic or democratic, leaders were at least predictable. Community, on the other hand, has a mind of its own.

Enterprises need to be building systems that support communities. Clearly industry is no longer about mass production or mass customization. Mass collaboration is the goal and challenge of the new economy.

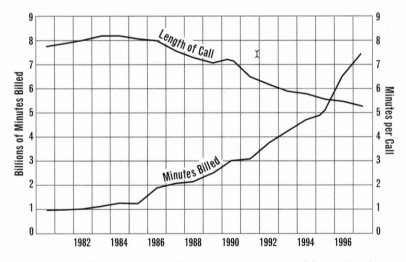

Figure 1.3 An inflection point can be seen at the beginning of the last decade, since which time the volume of telephone calls has increased by 300 percent while the average length of each call has dropped by nearly 30 percent. While by this time we may have been well into the information age, we can label this inflection point the beginning of age of info-glut. Imagine the manager forced to make three times as many more phone calls, but, choked with information, he has to cut each one shorter. Sound familiar? Also consider that despite the shorter calls, we are each spending three times the amount of time on the phone as we were a decade ago.

A headless organization—sounds like anathema doesn't it? Sure, especially if you're the head. Take heart: For the same reasons that we elect leaders of the free world, we'll still put people at the head of corporations. We will always need someone to blame when things go wrong.

Something has to give. Complexity cannot simply continue to increase without a change in the very engines that drive community, connectivity and commerce. And these engines are rooted deeply in much more than the recent advent of the dot coms.

Connecting the Dot-Coms: Building the X-Economy

It's far too easy to chalk up the advent of the X-economy to the dot-com phenomenon. Clearly it had its start long before the Internet. Communities have always been at the core of every industry in the form of associations, professional groups, and trade networks. The concept of electronic communications between communities of traders and individuals has been around since computers were born. As early as the 1960s, work was begun to enable both the transfer of data between multiple organizations and the sending and receiving of personal messages.

Electronic Data Interchange (EDI), commonly perceived as the forerunner of today's exchanges, was focused on the challenges of developing common data formats to enable data transfer, with Open Systems Integration (OSI) an outgrowth of this work. Early Internet developments laid the stage for a new era of cheap and ubiquitous means of interpersonal communications. The problem with both technologies was that they were cumbersome and non-intuitive. Technology professionals were needed to intervene even for routine transactions, while consumers were entirely left out of the electronic process.

To create the electronic marketplace, tools were needed that could be easily understood and used by virtually every buyer and seller, without technical worries. When the enabling Web technologies burst on the scene as an outgrowth of previous communications and software developments, the stage was set for a virtual explosion. Buyers and sellers could access data and send personal messaging. What's more, Web technologies offered ease of use, speed, and universal access. Anybody could use it—most importantly the consumer!

The advent of wide-area communications, combined with the Web, is creating new business processes and new value chains to compete with and through. At the heart of this transformation was something utterly simple, which began at the frontlines of the market where business meets consumers. At this touch point, the Web formed immediate connections between buyer and seller. Soon, like an inflating balloon, the increasing perimeter of the e-commerce market created enormous pressure on the value chain of myriad suppliers and service providers involved in each transaction to meet the new benchmark of immediacy.

> The X-economy is about much more than the notion of consumer-based Internet commerce. The innumerable Dotcom companies that once littered the market were just the eggshell-thin layer surrounding the X-economy.

Almost overnight, the "information float" in market interactions began to vanish as the pace of life accelerated. With little or no lag time in transactions, both buyers and sellers became ever more conscious of time. Today, buyers take for granted the ability to find information on goods and services at the click of a mouse; now sellers have to scramble to keep up. This attitudinal shift has filtered through the entire value chain. And it is this shift that, more than anything else, has brought the X-economy to center stage. Since it is no longer the realm of any one business to suit the needs of the consumer but rather a cacophony of interrelated business partners, coordination across each is essential to achieve competitive responsiveness.

Rapid advances in Internet technologies and the subsequent proliferation of economic activities on the Internet have ushered in a connected age where virtually every organization is trying to position itself to take advantage of new relationships within itself and between its customers and suppliers. This jockeying for advantage is dramatically altering and reconstituting the fundamental assumptions about markets and economics.

Yet the sheer magnitude of the discussion is daunting. The X-economy is about much more than the notion of consumer-based Internet commerce. The innumerable Dot-com companies that once littered the market were just the eggshell-thin layer surrounding the X-economy.

Consider a simple question that helps illustrate the scale of the X-economy: "How many companies were involved in the last consumer purchase you made?"

From your perspective the participants were limited to the businesses directly interacting with you. The complexity of the value chain that leads to an automobile's manufacture is not significant to you. As a consumer you simply want to know that the company and the person you are buying the product from possess all of the information necessary to stand behind the transaction, make it simple and cost-effective. The fact that Ford has more than 150,000 suppliers in its supply chain is of little interest to you.

Yet the intricacy of even the simplest of value chains involves an enormous amount of coordination in suppliers, partnerships, distribution channels, and intermediaries. Coordination that locks in partners, creates high transfer costs, and ultimately drives market inefficiency.

This inefficiency is reflected in fewer options for buyers and greater barriers for competitors. These are markets where large players have established impenetrable positions by virtually holding hostage the constituents of their supply chains.

The X-economy is the context for radically changing this model of the value chain by shifting the emphasis to a demand chain model where buyers drive the creation of new services and products. It will determine the cost, convenience, and complexity of nearly every transaction you participate in during your lifetime. And in just a few short years it will eclipse sectors such as energy, automobiles, and telecommunications with a new class of business that cater to building the exchange infrastructure for myriad communities of trade.

Yet most of this will be invisible to consumers and consumer markets. Like a giant perfumery that extracts a few precious drops of essence from acres of flowers, the X-economy is a distillery. What is visible to the end user is but a slight fraction of the enormous machinery in place to create the final product.

The New Engines of Commerce

Every aspect of business from manufacturing to marketing, promotion, distribution, and product creation will be affected by online exchanges. These new engines of commerce will drive the evolution of the free market in ways that we can hardly begin to comprehend. By connecting business partners, suppliers, and customers across what have been seemingly impenetrable boundaries of geography and industry, new levels of both innovation and competitiveness will emerge.

As competencies and innovations flow freely across market boundaries, the direction of the most radical change in the X-economy will most often be a surprise. In the same way that many important innovations tend to find the most fertile soil outside of the markets within which they were created. Rogaine, for example, which was originally a drug for managing high blood pressure but is now used to treat baldness, products and services will migrate to the markets where they have the greatest value.

In terms of our discussion about communities of trade, this means that there will be greater permeability between these communities as they share ideas through on line exchanges.

The inevitable fate of the free market lies in managing these increasingly complex communities of trade resulting from the incredible increase in the volume of transactions, the velocity of communication, and the increasingly shorter duration of opportunity. Yet there is nothing new about the basics of commerce.

Commerce, or the interchange of goods and commodities, has been a constant force in human society. From the ancient souk to the regional megamall, the fundamentals of commerce have remained the same: the principle of supply and demand; the quest for the best goods; the haggle for the fairest price; the search for reliable suppliers; the exchange of information and currency.

Despite these constants, the processes for conducting business are in constant flux. In this ebb and flow, power and advantage have shifted between buyers and suppliers in a cyclical pattern over time in response to production innovations, institutional, or political developments. For example, while early commercial transactions revolved around ad hoc personal interchanges between buyer and seller, by the late industrial economy, technological and industrial innovation had taken much of the personal out of the interchange, and in effect, migrated power substantially in the direction of the producer/supplier.

These foundation trends of the industrial economy and its organizational forms have been laid deeply into the culture of our businesses today, creating some of most significant problems that need to be overcome.

Simply put, as complexity of enterprises and markets increase, a means has to evolve by which to also increase efficiency.

Modern manufacturing initially created efficiencies in the factories, but set into motion complicated "front office" consequences, which led to today's mass sales and marketing approaches—from direct mail to big box outlets. Development of rapid transportation—from steam engine to jet plane—enabled international trade but created detailed regulations and trade procedures. Early communications innovations, such as the telephone, spurred the growth of huge national and international corporations along with great wealth, but promulgated a complex hierarchical management and sales structures.

By the mid-twentieth century, corporations had become little nations unto themselves, with customers often at their mercy. Information about products and services were released to buyers as the seller saw fit, with a subsequent breakdown of interchange between buyer and seller. This was the era that saw the most pronounced rise of the middleman and the creation of the bureaucracy of business—both legacies we have struggled with through to the present day. Even after the initial introduction of computers, much of the dynamic nature of commerce was lost under piles of paper and often "Dilbertesque" procedures. Enter Information Technology with its promise to change all of this by disintermediating business and once again connecting buyers and seller. Yet, as we have seen with the near collapse of the dotcom phenomenon, it's not as easy in the real world as it appears in a business plan.

Disintermediation unchecked wreaks havoc on marketplaces. There are far too many options in the way of suppliers, products, and services; too many ways to sew all of these options together; and too much complexity in managing even the simplest supply chain to eliminate the role of intermediaries. Exchanges are more than a means of disintermediation; more than just a technology fix. What's needed is nothing less than a new way to form communities.

As of the writing of this book, more than 1,000 online exchanges exist. These are *communities* of trade where instant enterprises can be formed. Transactions happen in a near frictionless environment. And demand drives the formation of products and services that no genius marketer or focus group could ever have predicted.

Simply put, as complexity of enterprises and markets increase, a means has to evolve by which to also increase efficiency (see Figure 1.4). Online exchanges are that evolution.

Here are just a few examples of these new marketplaces:

- *Intel* has blazed its way into the Internet economy, selling almost $1 billion a month (or about 50 percent of revenues) on the Web—in products ranging from chips to motherboards. It transacts business via personalized Web sites with 550 original equipment manufacturers and distributors in 46 countries.
- *Enron,* owner of EnronOnline, where more than 900 products are traded. It's the world's first Web-based system enabling companies to buy and sell the full range of wholesale energy products online.
- *Covisint,* an alliance among GM, Ford, Daimler-Chrysler, Renault, and Nissan expects to generate up $500 billion in transactions for automotive industry purchasing.
- *Trade-ranger* joins the forces of 14 energy and petrochemical companies including Royal Dutch/Shell, BP Amoco, Conoco, Dow Chemical, Equilon Enterprises, Mitsubishi Corporation,

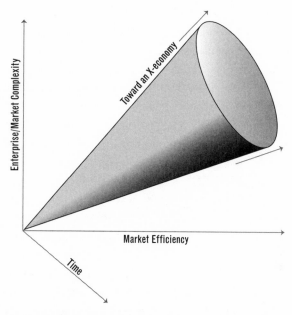

Figure 1.4   If we plot the increasing complexity of markets, products, and enterprise over time, it becomes clear that the efficiency of the market must also increase to accommodate this complexity. X-economy exchanges are one significant way to synchronize these two dynamics, complexity, and efficiency.

Motiva Enterprises, Occidental Petroleum, Phillips Petroleum, Repsol YPF, Statoil, Tosco, TotalFinaElf, and Unocal in a global exchange that accounts for $125 billion in expenditures.

- *GlobalNetExchange* is positioning itself in the retail space with founders Sears, Carrefour, Metro AG, and Kroger to funnel $158 billion in purchasing.
- Union Pacific Corp., CSX Corp., Norfolk Southern Corp., and Canadian Pacific Ltd., have each invested in *Arzoon*, an exchange for rail customers to procure, execute, and track freight movements.
- *Burlington Northern Santa Fe* created a subsidiary called FreightWise Inc. to provide an online marketplace for buyers and sellers of transportation services.

- *BuyerZone.com* has already facilitated over $2.5 billion in purchases by small businesses through its indirect catalog and Request for Proposal distribution service.
- *Logistics.com* has increased liquidity in the fragmented transportation market by facilitating 2.4 million transactions per year by 2000 representing $1.7 billion in freight volume.
- *FreeMarkets* in 1999, the same year many exchanges were just starting to deploy, executed over $2.7 billion in reverse auctions for buyers who are estimated to have saved in excess of $350 million.
- *Ingram Micro* with 140,000 resellers in 130 countries is the world's largest technology products distributor and has an on-line ordering system that can support more than 70 million transactions a day.
- *Owens & Minor,* a $3 billion company based in Virginia, is the largest U.S. distributor of medical and surgical supplies to hospitals, integrated healthcare systems, and group purchasing organizations worldwide. Its exchange allows company to sit in the middle of the supply chain and share information on both sides. It also allows suppliers to analyze product-purchasing patterns to better forecast demands.

> Demand drives the formation of products and services that no genius marketer or focus group could ever have predicted.

And these are just a handful of the marketplaces in place today. As we will discuss later, some will become role models for success in the X-economy but many will fail as they try to define this new model of business. Nonetheless, within the next five years, transactions in these marketplaces will account for more than 10 percent of worldwide GDP. Although that may be difficult to accept consider that Microsoft recently purchased the rights to 80,000 marketplaces. This would allow Microsoft to build, giveaway, sell, or otherwise deploy 80,000 online exchanges for everything from fishing lures to aircraft engines.

Microsoft's move is the historical equivalent of the Louisiana purchase, representing a nearly two-fold order of magnitude increase in the current number of exchanges. And that's just one datapoint—albeit an enormous one. In every industry there are innumerable opportunities for exchanges to spring up. Again, let's be clear here. We do not think that most of these marketplaces will survive. In fact, we do not believe that most deserve to survive, but that does not make the phenomenon any less spectacular.

In large part what we see happening with online exchanges is evolution at its best—shifting through a massive selection of the fittest. We fail to consider that evolution is a very inefficient process. The key in evolving any complex organism is incurring an overwhelming preponderance of failure. From a competitive vantage point, failure is as necessary in the evolution of the free market as it is in the evolution of biological organisms. However, given the degree of sudden adaptation required on the part of virtually all supply chains, it is likely that both evolution and the rate of failure will increase.

Organizations building on line exchanges or participating in them find themselves in a particularly precarious spot where the old business models for partnering are beginning to fail and yet the new models for the X-economy are still unknown. (More on this in Chapter 3.)

Moreover, at the same time that these exchanges are taking shape, unprecedented availability of capital is fueling even greater levels of innovation and entrepreneurship across all industries.

It is probably this combination of velocity, opportunity, and the inevitability of some new, as of yet unforeseen, framework of the X-economy that simultaneously frightens and attracts most of us.

> The key in evolving any complex organism is incurring an overwhelming preponderance of failure. From a competitive vantage point failure is as necessary in the evolution of the free market as it is in the evolution of biological organisms.

This framework for the X-economy is based on the simple principle of using exchanges to build instant community—eliminating the lag time involved in the formation of any organization or market.[4]

As a result of its enabling technologies and business models, the X-economy:

- Opens markets to all available participants.
- Accelerates markets and innovation.
- Increases market efficiency.
- Creates demand-driven markets.

The X-economy Opens Markets

Certainly free markets have *always* encouraged diversity, choice, and evolution. And this has lead to an ever-increasing number of new opportunities for enterprise. But, as with any evolutionary system, the pace of change in free markets accelerates as time progresses—making the need to respond increasingly more important as a survival tactic.

The manner in which any system, biologic or economic, manages this rate of accelerating creation is by balancing increasing complexity with increasing efficiency. As the stuff of innovation becomes easier and faster to come by, the complexity required to support the next wave of innovation must increase at least as fast.

The X-economy Accelerates Innovation

The problem is that we have long associated speed of innovation with the size of the organization (i.e., small is fast). That works when the value chains of a large enterprise are rigid and not easily reformed to meet the demands of the market. In addition, it is common knowledge that large value chains, for instance, the sort used in the automotive industry, create insurmountable barriers to entry for new players.

---

[4] Although we prefer the concept of community to that of markets, when describing the X-economy, it is easiest to begin by using existing paradigms such as markets to begin our discussion of the X-economy's transformation.

The X-Economy Increases Market Efficiency

But what if we were able to create value chains instantly? What if all businesses, no matter how large, were nothing more than an infinitely malleable and instantly responsive universe of small businesses?

A basic tenet of the X-economy is that size does not determine speed. Speed is determined by time-to-community. And, unlike the behemoth integrated value chains of the past, these newer communities do not speak to the rigid, controlled supply chains popularized in the better portion of the twentieth century. Instead they consist of constantly, instantly shifting relationships among community members. Because of this, size alone does not define community ownership—it is no longer justifiable for the largest player to own the largest supply chain. The communities are instead owned by their members, something we will talk more about in Chapter 3, when we explore the various types of trading communities.

> The framework for the X-economy is based on the simple principle of using exchanges to build instant community—eliminating the lag time involved in the formation of any organization or market.

Therefore, the faster you can create a community of suppliers, partners, and distributors to respond to a demand the more likely you are to succeed—as a community and as a part of it.

Sounds simple, right? Sure, until you get mired in the myriad tasks involved in forming a community, from identifying partners to negotiating terms and contracts to justifying the costs of building each new value chain. This is why large businesses still dominate markets in the face of enormous market inefficiency. In short, traditional value chains have created insurmountable barriers to innovation and evolution. (Hard way to learn this lesson: Try to compete against an industry behemoth. Easy way to learn this lesson: Pick up any of Michael Porter's books and you'll get all the education you need on this topic.)

Here is where the rules change—in a big way.

The X-Economy Creates Demand-Driven Markets

The X-economy represents a new mechanism for establishing markets at this new level of complexity through a series of exchanges in which trading communities are increasingly being formed. These exchanges are catalysts for a new marketplace much more complex and far more sophisticated than anything our traditional business institutions are prepared for. Exchanges are likely to be the greatest value proposition for new business and the central metaphor for the way all business is conducted over the next hundred years. Most importantly, they will erode the bedrock of traditional value chains and open the doors to a new era of entrepreneurship.

The Path from Innovation to Construction

Why are exchanges so important to the X-economy? In complex markets, such as automobile manufacturing, there are a multitude of transactions and mechanisms to form and manage value chains that are as complex and as well-entrenched as the tributary system of the Nile. A seemingly endless cascade of suppliers goes into the production of an automobile. And the path from innovation to the construction of any new model requires an enormous amount of time and effort to establish a new value chain of partners, suppliers, and distributors.

This also assumes that all of the buyers and sellers in any marketplace are known to each other. That is clearly not the case since much of the effort that any business is engaged in involved promoting, marketing, and selling its services or products to organizations who needs its goods but are not familiar with it. (Refer to Figure 1.5.)

Now, suppose it were possible to remove all of the tedium, market and pricing inefficiency, and process latency involved in the chain of

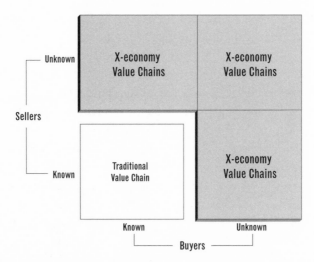

Figure 1.5   The majority of interactions between buyers and sellers result from established networks, alliances, and communities of trade. Yet in every industry the preponderance of possible buyers or sellers is unknown, due to factors ranging from geography to new and innovative entrants. In an X-economy the barriers of participation are removed for all buyers and sellers.

events required to identify, qualify, and engage with partners across all four of our quadrants? What if we were to remove the transactions from the process and instantly coordinate the community of providers and suppliers (current and potential) based on the demand side rather than the supply side of the industry? The result would be an extraordinary increase in the velocity of innovation and market efficiency—not to mention a flood of new enterprise.

The Myth of Disintermediation

In the case of every major economic or social shift, there seems to be a central myth to be dispelled. In the case of the X-economy, the central theme to be exorcised is that the middleman will become extinct.

This is not a new business proposition. One of the most visible examples of the interplay between disintermediation, efficiency and the economy is more than 100 years old, Sears, Roebuck and Co.

According to Sears, "By the time Sears was started, farmers in rural America were selling their crops for cash and buying what they needed from rural general stores. But when they laid their money on the line for goods, farmers saw red. In 1891, the wholesale price of a barrel of flour was reported to be $3.47. Price at retail was at least $7, a 100 percent increase. Farmers formed protest movements, such as the Grange, to do battle against high prices and the middleman."

It is worth noting that the infrastructure that made the Sears' catalog possible was the burgeoning railroad system. Sears founder, Richard Sears, was a railroad agent who accidentally received a shipment of goods bound for a jeweler. When the jeweler decided he did not want the shipment, Sears bought the goods himself and resold them—eliminating the local middleman. From this Sears created his own network of agents through which to deliver all manner of goods. (Might this be an appropriate analogy for the infrastructure effect of the Internet on X-economy exchanges?)

Everything from headware to headstones could be purchased through the Sears catalog at what was promised to be the "price your storekeeper at home pays for everything . . . and will prevent him from overcharging you" (Figures 1.6 and 1.7).

Sears grew dramatically as did consumerism. And, despite the apparent threat of disintermediation the retail industry flourished. The easiest way to understand this phenomenon and its application to the X-economy is to use a simple framework to describe the relationship between the increasing market complexity and increasing market efficiency. An economy consists of the basic interactions involved in exchanging products between buyers and sellers. As an economy matures its products and markets get more complex. If the market's efficiency, that is the ability of the buyers to have fast access to competitive alternatives, does not also increase the economy stalls; it cannot grow. On the other hand, if its efficiency increases the economy grows.

The Sears catalog was a mechanism by which to increase market efficiency in an era of increasingly greater complexity of transportation systems, product alternatives, and more widely distributed populous outside of the city. As was the case with these early catalogs, one of the greatest early economic promises of computers, and more specifically

Figure 1.6   The Sears Catalog promised to disintermediate retail markets. But, rather than crush the retail industry, it heralded an age of amazing increases in consumerism.

Figure 1.7 Everything from headware to headstones could be purchased through the Sears Catalog at what was promised to be the "price your storekeeper at home pays for everything . . . and will prevent him from overcharging you."

the Internet, was that market efficiency would increase due to the shift from intermediation to disintermediation. That is, the shift from an economy of many middlemen to an economy where transactions occurred directly between buyer and seller. It seemed to make sense that fewer participants in the value chain would streamline markets. Examples such as Dell computer seemed to reinforce this notion with the great success they have had selling computers directly to consumers.

That was a textbook example of oversimplification. The reality was that as the number of products and potential interactions in value chains increased rapidly and as markets globalized to include countless new providers and buyers, the complexity of the interactions and competitive alternatives increased just as dramatically. As manufacturers who travel down the path to disintermediation quickly learned, intermediaries are very often necessary to translate market demand into customized products. The indirect channel offers layers of localized knowledge that are a critical component to successfully transforming horizontal products in vertical solutions. The X-economy is not about disintermediation. Instead it is about re-intermediation where new technologies make it possible to commensurately increase both complexity and efficiency with the introduction of new marketplaces. In these markets, value chains are constantly reforming as quickly as the demands of the consumer and of the business change. In large part this is made possible by the Internet, and the ready infrastructure it offers for innovation.

> In the past, markets turned like large boats in slow arcs as ideas were translated into a long series of new innovations needed for their success. Today's markets turn on a dime as ideas take root in a super-fertile infrastructure.

Unlike many of the technologies that have preceded it, from the advent of telephone, radio, and cable television to the use of electronic data interchange (EDI), the infrastructure for the X-economy is already in place. There is no information superhighway to be built. The roads for the adoption of exchanges are already well paved. And unlike the proverbial cow paths, these roadways are agile, malleable thorough-fares that respond easily to changing market dynamics. Virtually every significant aspect of the X-economy's technology framework is in place and waiting to be exploited by a free market hungry for innova-tive velocity and growth.

The effect is something for which mankind's technological prog-ress has no precedent. With the innovation of every previous techno-logical marvel an era of infrastructure building had to follow. From the wiring of the globe necessary for early telecommunication to the creation of orbital rocketry for a global satellite networks, to the evo-lution of factory precision for creation of the turbine engines that power modern air transport, decades have always stood between the idea and the promise.

In the past, markets turned like large boats in slow arcs as ideas were translated into a long series of new innovations needed for their success. Today's markets turn on a dime as ideas take root in a super-fertile infrastructure. The only obstacle is the tolerance of our own behaviors and willingness to change—but even this seems to be fast eroding in the face of unprecedented competitive pressure.

Creative Destruction

Political economist Joseph Schumpeter's articulation of the creative destruction process in capitalist economies makes an appropriate epi-graph for today's X-economy transformations.

> . . . in capitalist reality as distinguished from its textbook picture, it is not (price) competition which counts but the competition from the new com-modity, the new technology, the new source of supply, the new type of or-ganization(the largest scale unit of control for instance)—competition which commands a decisive cost or quality advantage and which strikes not at the margins of the profits and the outputs of the existing firms but at their foundations and their very lives. . . . It is hardly necessary to point

out that competition of the kind we now have in mind acts not only when in being but also when it is merely an ever-present threat. It disciplines before it attacks. (Joseph Schumpeter: *Capitalism, Socialism and Democracy*, 1942.)

The first step in creating any new economic, political, or social system is arguably the most radical and tumultuous—deconstruction of the existing system. Something needs to disturb the balance of power and credibility of the existing system that movement to a new system seems painless by contrast, inevitable, even though the precise nature of that new system may be far from clear.

We would argue that the greatest force of creative destruction in today's markets is the dis-integration of organizations. The steady shift towards focusing on core competency and outsourcing everything else has had a profound effect on the very notion of an organization. Although the continued mania in mergers and acquisitions has created an illusion of ever-increasing large enterprise, it masks the even faster acceleration of entrepreneurship, access to capital and small business. The result has been a shift to a much more granular economy.

At the same time, partnering in the form of coopetition, strategic alliances, contracting, and service providers has risen just as steeply. The result of these two dynamics has been the decomposition of monolithic enterprise into a fertile soil for the formation of spontaneous coalitions.

While the economy used to resemble a fairly linear pyramid of small, mid-sized, and large business, the X-economy looks more like a hyperbolic pyramid (see Figure 1.8) where the velocity of small business is expanding far more rapidly than that of large enterprise at the top of the pyramid. Exchanges are a key factor in this.

We would go so far as to propose that exchanges are an absolute necessity for continued economic prosperity. As markets, enterprises, and distribution channels rapidly dis-integrate, on line exchanges are a requisite mechanism for coordinating this quantum increase in the complexity of the economy. We realize that this sort of discussion opens the door to a classic chicken and egg debate. Are exchanges leading to complexity or is complexity leading to exchanges? This may

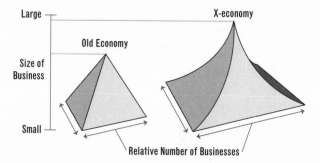

Figure 1.8 The X-economy creates a fertile environment for dis-integration where smaller enterprises can quickly form supply chains with each other or with larger companies. This does not eliminate the role of large multinational enterprises but it does create greater acceleration and opportunity for innovation among small businesses. It also provides an important counterbalance to the merger mania that would otherwise result in only a few multinationals devouring all industries.

appear to be a meaningless and pedantic pursuit, but we believe it does help to shed light on the underlying factors that extend well beyond the X-economy and are reshaping all forms of social institutions.

Are the individual participants in the economy's value chains—today's successful businesses—likely to stand by while wholesale decimation takes place before their very eyes?

If we look to biology as an analogy it is clear that all life tends toward greater complexity and diversity as it evolves. In the case of intelligent life, evolution has resulted in ever more complex organisms and collections of organisms. Keeping pace with this complexity has required sophisticated nervous systems and social orders. For intelligent life, this often translates into embedded intelligence that governs community interactions—call it *instinct*.

We would claim that exchanges represent a form of intelligence for an economy that allow it to evolve to greater levels of complex, intelligent behavior.

It's clear, however, that not all organizations are evolving at the same rate. For those slower to dis-integrate, exchanges tear down the walls placed between the parts of an organization, its people, its suppliers, its customers, and potentially all the relationships in its vital value chain.

But consider: These walls placed between people, partners, and processes have been constructed at great sacrifice over years of business development to compartmentalize and protect competitive positions relative to the buying preferences of carefully identified customers. Are the individual participants in the economy's value chains—today's successful businesses—likely to stand by while wholesale decimation takes place before their very eyes?

In fact, in the development of business over the past century, such transformative changes have taken place over and over again. The only difference this time is the Internet speed with which the impact will be felt.

Take as one example the monopolies created at the end of the nineteenth and the beginning of the twentieth century by the activities of the "robber barons" in iron, railroad, real estate, and natural resources industries. They built enormous, integrated, value-chained structures to insure the operating standards, scale, and, not incidentally, profitability desirable to minimize competitive risks. These relationships were built on the principle of locking in partners as part of an impenetrable value chain.

Ultimately these kinds of barriers to competition have not been sustained. Although interventions via judicial action or legislative deregulation may hasten the demise of any dominant regime in the economy, the underlying dynamic has consistently shown that a free market will erode uncompetitive structures as new forces seize on technology change and specialized components of the value chain innovate around the largest of syndicates.

In very practical terms, surviving the freefall from evolution is a matter of first establishing a set of reference points, which can then be used to gauge how much and how fast we need to change our current business practices.

As we will see in the coming chapters, the X-economy may be in a state of chaos but it has a clear set of rules and frameworks that will work just as well for these new businesses as those of the industrial era did for their counterparts.

But don't forget something we said earlier, "Simple rules do not a simple world make." Systems can still be dauntingly complex in their interactions, connections, velocity, and volume and yet be governed by very simple rules. DNA contains the blueprint for all life, yet it consists of only four base amino acids that can only be paired according to relentless precision, yet the systems that result are anything but simple.

Value Chain Analysis in the X-Economy

It is impossible to go much further in our discussion without first describing in more detail what we mean by the term value chain and a bit of its history. The concept of the value chain has become an immutable law of business and, more specifically, competition. Originally developed by Michael Porter, author of *Competitive Advantage,* the basic idea is that a value chain represents the collective partnerships, resources, and processes that bring a product or service to market.

From Porter's view, the entity at the center of competition is not necessarily the traditional notion of an organization defined in terms of physical resources such as buildings, factories, and employees, but rather the collection of all the activities that are combined to create value. This collection of value creating activities is the *value chain.*

The Role of External Linkages

Porter's premise was simple: By maximizing the efficiency of a value chain, costs go down and differentiation goes up, and from this movement competitive advantage is created. Porter's work was rooted in the study of *transaction cost economics,* which looked at organizations as the series of activities (what we now describe now as the value chain) and sought to assess the relative costs of performing and coordinating them.

Earlier economists, such as R. H. Coase and later Oliver Williamson, focused heavily on the costs of performing activities internally versus partnering or outsourcing them. In their time, information technology was at its infancy and as a result the transaction costs involved in the coordination of value chain externalities where much higher than today. As a result, their conclusion in almost every case was to perform these tasks in-house.

This type of thinking leads to the notion of vertical integration, where (it is assumed) competitive advantage comes from total control over every aspect of the value chain. Think of Henry Ford, with his vision of the factory village where iron ore would enter one end and a complete automobile would come out the other. It is this model of vertical integration that defined the old economy—where everything fit on one balance sheet, from the sheep that produced the wool to weave car seats, to the steel foundries that created raw metal to the stamping machines that formed it into car parts.

Other examples from early twentieth century abound. For instance, the oil industry was built on a model where everything from exploration to retail delivery of oil products was controlled by large integrated suppliers from J. D. Rockefeller's Standard Oil to present day behemoths such as Chevron, Shell, Exxon, and Mobil. Even more modern industries such information technology had, at least early on, relied heavily on a model vertical integration. Think of the IBM mainframe, where every aspect of design and production was controlled and owned by IBM, from the internal components to the software that ran on it. Early competitors such as Honeywell, Unisys, and General Dynamics promoted the same Byzantine models governed by the notion the "not invented here" was an anathema.

Today, however, the cost of maintaining vertically integrated infrastructure is more often than not greater than the cost of coordinating external value chain. As a result, the notion of value chain integration has been steadily eroding over the past four decades. Today, in virtually every industry, partnering across the value chain has become the norm. In the oil industry, large players such as Chevron now buy the majority of their oil from other sources and distribute the majority of their gasoline through third-party retail outlets.

IBM, as does the entire computer industry, now relies heavily on third parties for software, electronic components, and services. In fact, today, it is likely that IBM receives the majority of its revenue through external value chain activities. (This is not something that they reveal externally or perhaps know for sure themselves, but even a cursory look at their financial statements indicates this is very likely the case.)

This is not to say that IBM is the computer industry's role model for leveraging value creation outside of its org chart. To the contrary, IBM remains one of the most vertically integrated amongst its peers. Rather we point out this incremental but significant shift at IBM to illustrate how important external activities have become to the notion of the value chain and the ability to sustain competitive advantage.

Advances in information technology have drastically reduced transaction costs between external activities and, in effect, reversed the early propositions of Coase and Williamson. However, do not lose sight of just how important this point is. As transaction costs move toward zero, the traditional notion of the corporation becomes irrelevant and the role of the value chain becomes omnipotent. In essence, this is the basis of this entire book. We are today in the midst of a sea change in the how we relate to markets, partners, and customers. If we do not examine and learn from the lessons of recent history, we are all but guaranteed to repeat the same mistakes.

The key to sustaining competitive advantage has shifted from vertical integration to managing value creating activities external to the organization.

During the first half of this century, the notion of *economy of scale* dominated thinking on competitive advantage. The degree of competitiveness was measured in terms of how vertically integrated an organization could be and the degree of top-down control it could exert over individual value creating activities. In simple terms, economy of scale is the ability to derive greater value from one large entity than a collection of smaller ones. And it is this notion that drove the design of value chains, and, in many cases, organizations themselves.

Consider GM, the philosophical successor to Ford and the standard-bearer of vertical integration for many decades. Pick up a copy of Forbes or Fortune from the 1950s or 1960s and it will likely be filled with gushing praise for GM and its management. The economy of scale for GM was so great, how could it ever lose?

GM was the most admired company in America, if not the world, for decades. During these golden years in the middle of this century, GM could do no wrong in the eyes of the business press and management pundits. Ironic then, that GM has consistently lost market share every year for the past three decades. What went wrong? The answer lies not in size but in speed.

From Scale to Speed

At the outbreak of World War II, the U.S. government mobilized U.S. manufacturing into a war machine by turning to the auto industry for the production of war materials. At that time a B-24 plant in California, the heart of aircraft production, was producing one bomber per day operating under optimum conditions. Henry Ford's Willow Run plant in Ypsilanti, Michigan used auto industry production-line techniques that allowed Ford to produce one B-24 Liberator bomber per hour!

Over the course of little more than a year, the U.S. revolutionized not only *what* it was producing, but *how* it was produced. Relative to the benchmarks of the era, this was turning on a dime. Unfortunately, it required a crisis the size of WW II to force a change of this magnitude. Fortunately for mankind, there has since been no other crisis's of this magnitude to inspire such sudden change. But the trend has clearly continued, far from where it began.

For the last five decades there has been a subtle shift from "econ-omy of scale" to "economy of speed." This has been driven in large part by the emergence of information technology and other resources that increased the efficiency and effectiveness by which organizations are able to communicate and coordinate value chain activities.

The U.S. auto industry was an early adopter of these technologies. Electronic Data Interchange (EDI), which enable more efficient com-munication among trading partners. However, this early dabbling did little to change the behemoth, vertically integrated structures of the U.S. auto manufacturers. In fact it served only to hardwire its external partners into the organizational structure, obviated many of the bene-fits of an agile value chain. As a result, during the 1970s and 1980s we watched how vulnerable this industry was to the outside threat of or-ganizations that focused on *speed over scale.*

> Investments in technologies such as EDI helped to re-duce transaction costs involved with coordinating external value chain activities, but in most cases also further en-trenched partners into the vertically integrated organiza-tional structures.

During this time, Japanese auto manufacturers rapidly expanded their share of U.S. auto sales, at the expense of GM, Ford, and Chrysler (not to mention AMC and the few other smaller U.S. manufacturers who failed to survive this period). While the high-level process flows of building cars in Japan varied little from that of the United States, there were significant differences among the structure of their value chains during this time. Rather than seeking to assemble all compo-nents of the value chain under one roof or on a single balance sheet, Japanese manufacturers organized value chains into *keiretsu* or the coalitions of suppliers, manufacturers, and distributors that we now associate with complex industries such as auto manufacturing.

A series of subtle demographic shifts that over time allowed Japan to reshape itself according to the desires of the U.S. market, rather than to try to mold the market into its own image. Think speed over scale, as well as fluidity over momentum.

By dis-integrating the activities into parallel yet independent operations, Japanese manufacturers operated more efficiently than their U.S. counterparts, benefiting from advantageous capital structures enabled by having been freed from the burden of financing the entire value chain, for example. But the real source of competitive advantage, however, is derived from the greater speed of responsiveness to shifts in market demand that this model enables.

Most of the credit for Japan's early success in the U.S. auto market is given to the combined U.S. recession and energy crisis, resulting in a rapid shift of market demand that favored cheaper, fuel-efficient cars. If this were the only factor, however, it would have not been Japan but Volkswagen, with its more established distribution channel and greater brand recognition, to have victoriously emerged from this economic environment. But the reality is that this notion of a sea change in buyer behavior is greatly overstated. What actually happened was a series of subtle demographic shifts that over time allowed Japan to reshape itself according to the desires of the U.S. market, rather than to try to mold the market into its own image. Think speed over scale, as well as fluidity over momentum.

In the decade it took the U.S. auto industry to shift production from the gas guzzlers of the 1960s to the fuel efficient models only successfully introduced in the early 1980s, Japan had achieved several milestones in auto marketing and manufacturing to which their U.S. counterparts took years to respond to. These include:

1. Redefining the benchmark for product quality, away from the U.S. manufacturers' notion of planned obsolescence;

2. Establishing a new "economy" class of car marketed on the basis of preference rather than necessity;
3. Defining the "mid-size" category typified by the *Honda Accord* for which America was unable to respond to until the introduction of the *Ford Taurus*, almost a decade later; as well as,
4. Introducing "light trucks" as a new class of vehicle that rapidly eroded the last sacred cow of the U.S. auto industry, the high margin business of building trucks (a segment previously untroubled by the notion of innovation or R&D).

These changes in strategic directions were not a function of the Japanese *kaizen* concept of incremental change. Rather in each case they represented an absolute redefinition of previous paradigms. As a result, responding to these opportunities required widespread changes in strategy and direction.

Herein lies the crux of the story—the success in these categories by Japanese auto manufacturers was not based on scale (e.g., the ability to produce the same product at a cheaper rate) or on the basis of a proprietary idea. In every case, American manufacturers held the advantage of greater scale and in many cases already had initiatives in place to rival those of their Japanese competitors. The real secret of their success was the ability of Japan to get products to market faster.

By rallying the constituents in their value chain, Japanese auto manufacturers were able to compress the time-to-market of new products to a fraction of that of their competitors. By being first to market in each category, they were able to establish the benchmark for each segment and shift turn the table on competitors by forcing them to respond to them. The result has been that in each category where Japan has brought a product to market first, it has consistently led in market share, while others have seen market share erode in other categories during the time they have spent responding to these new threats.

For example, while U.S. auto manufacturers have never been able to match Japan in the sale of economy class vehicles, it has been the largest producer of minivans and SUVs since the introduction of these categories in the 1980s (which combined, arguably saved the U.S. auto industry). By seeking to compete in this Japanese-dominated category rather acquiescing in favor of the segments where it is stronger, however, U.S. auto manufacturers have consistently seen their market share drop each year in the categories where they have led. By leveraging its superior responsiveness early in the cycle of new product introduction, Japan has been able to set the agenda in its favor and force competitors to respond to it.

From Vertical Integration to Organizational Dis-Integration

The ability of Japanese auto manufacturers to respond faster than their U.S. counterparts was a function of manipulating the composition of the value chain in a way to maximized speed of innovation, at a time when others were focusing on cost. However, it was not as though other competitors were entirely insensitive to the importance of time-to-market; rather, it was a matter of the organizational structure that defined the decision process for these value chains impeding the rate of innovation and responsiveness.

As observed by Klaus Schwab, founder and president of the World Economic Forum, "We are moving from a world in which the big eat the small to a world in which the fast eat the slow." A flip assessment of the problem facing U.S. auto manufacturers might be that size alone was the problem—these organizations are just too big. But the fact is that size alone does not determine speed. While smaller organizations are typically quicker to respond than larger ones, small stature does not guarantee a responsive value chain. Speed in the X-economy is determined by the rate at which a responsive value chain can be assembled, a rate that we have termed *time-to-community*.

What impact does the rate of time-to-community have on a market? To appreciate the answer, consider for a moment the notion of any business not as a vertically integrated organization, but instead as a collection of an infinitely malleable and instantly responsive universe of independently operating small businesses. Each of these businesses focuses on its own area of core competency and spends all its resources on producing value in this area in the most expedient manner possible, and none on dealing with the politics and Byzantine organizational structure of a large organization. Now imagine the ability to address each opportunity by assembling the right combination of these small businesses and instantly being able to communicate, coordinate, and respond appropriately.

> We are moving from a world in which the big eat the small to a world in which the fast eat the slow.

Far fetched? Perhaps, in the context of the old economy. But so, too, had been the notion of using information technology to work with suppliers to have just the amount of inventory needed on hand at a given moment, rather than ordering days in advance as was done for centuries of manufacturing. This is the notion of just-in-time (JIT) inventory which today is a component of most large value chains, but which was a revolutionary concept when introduced just a few decades ago (another area of Japanese innovation).

In the X-economy, we are building JIT value chains with the ability to develop a community of partners that respond to a market's demands in the same way that JIT inventory anticipates production demands. In this lightening-paced competitive environment, sellers no longer have the luxury of pushing selected information to the buyer. To survive, they must quickly learn what buyers want. They must be able to react instantly, changing the product mix, prices, terms, and marketing message to suit each buyer. When buyers ask questions, they must have the ability to pull information from a wide range of company resources. Plus, sellers must develop secure methods to complete transactions and reliable methods for rapid fulfillment.

It is important, however, not to oversimplify the concept of the value chain and confuse the basic information exchanges associated with JIT inventory systems with the coordination of the complex information channels that define business. Value chain management is not simply a matter of providing "plumbing" between partners, but rather it is a holistic approach to the entire business cycle. The linkages of the value chain are the interdependent relationships of all value creating activities, not the point-to-point exchanges between buyer and seller or supplier and manufacturer.

> Consider for a moment the notion of any business not as a vertically integrated organization, by but instead as a collection of an infinitely malleable and instantly responsive universe of independently operating small businesses. Now imagine the ability to address each opportunity by assembling the right combination of these small businesses and instantly being able to communicate, coordinate, and respond appropriately.

To uncover where to dis-integrate value chain components and where to create linkages with external entities, it is important to provide answers to the following questions about activities along the value chain:

- Is the activity central to value creation or does it support other value creating activities?
- Is the activity easily interchangeable with new trading partners?
- Can the activity be outsourced with losing control of proprietary knowledge?
- Does the activity facilitate greater competition among suppliers?
- Does the activity demonstrably effect business cycle time or reducing time-to-community?
- Does the activity effect strategic linkages to customers and partners?
- Can the activity adapt "on the fly" as business conditions change?
- Is the activity a function of local conditions or market-wide dynamics?

These questions should be applied to the value chain analysis of the company, its customers, known competitors, and potential new entrants. This perspective provides the context for how competitive advantage is created through participation in or the development of an exchange. For example, if an exchange is used to coordinate activities in such a way as to speed the design process, competitive advantage is created. However if it also incorporates linkages to other activities, such as marketing and business development, this competitive advantage will be notably strengthened. Careful coordination of linkages can be a powerful source of competitive advantage by allowing the business to move faster than potential rivals are able to respond.

At first glance it may seen that the model for X-economy value chains is indistinguishable from a model for the old economy. We know human beings have been trading information, negotiating, completing transactions, and fulfilling business obligations since the beginning of recorded history. What is revolutionary about the X-economy, however, is the velocity and volume of exchanges, and the amount and accessibility of information available to both buyer and seller about the market.

For example, there is virtually no "information float" in the new exchange environment." Enabled by high-speed networks and Web technologies, buyers take for granted the ability to find information on goods and services. With a click of a mouse, they can compare features, prices, and terms. Fueled and empowered by market knowledge, buyers have a new control and autonomy in the purchase decision. Indeed, the hub of the commerce process shifts more towards the buyer and less towards the selling organization.

In this lightening-paced competitive environment, sellers no longer have the luxury of pushing selected information to the buyer. To survive, they must quickly learn what buyers want. They must be able to react instantly, changing the product mix, prices, terms, and marketing message to suit each buyer. When buyers ask questions, they must have the ability to pull information from a wide range of company resources. Plus, sellers must develop secure methods to complete transactions and reliable methods for rapid fulfillment.

However, managing an exchange and optimizing its value chain is not simply a matter of high-speed plumbing. The infrastructure is only the foundation for changes that will ripple through all aspects of business, culture, trust, and communities that form the building blocks of the X-economy.

The Father of the X-Economy

In fact, the whole world may be looked upon as a vast general market made up of diverse special markets where social wealth is bought and sold. Our task then is to discover the laws to which these purchases and sales tend to conform automatically. To this end, we shall suppose that the market is perfectly competitive, just as in pure mechanics we suppose to start with, that machines are perfectly frictionless.

Léon Walras, *Elements of Pure Economics,* 1874: p. 84

We must end this first chapter with a short footnote about the individual who we believe first gave shape and substance to the concept of market exchanges. Although unknown to most, Léon Walras (pronounced Val′ros) is considered by many to be one of the most influential economists of the industrial age.

Walras (1834–1910) was a French economist who was among the original "marginalists," a group of economists who created modern economics by shifting the focus of price theory from the supplier (costs) to the consumer (value). Sound familiar? Walras is given credit for originating the theory of diminishing marginal utility of a good.[5] That is simply, the more you have of something the less you value additional units of it. Sounds simple, but then again the fundamentals of economics usually are. It is the translation of these basics into an understanding of the behaviors of complex markets that confounds us.

Walras also tried to explain how not just some transactions or markets but *all* markets must clear at socially acceptable prices. It's one thing to say that individuals can achieve a price mutually acceptable to both a buyer (who wants to pay less) and a supplier (who wants to charge more). But Walras claimed that not just individual transactions will be efficient but all transactions across the entire economy will be efficient.

A mathematician, Walras understood that if each market cleared at an efficient price (what he termed *tatonnement*), then the markets

---

[5] The theory of marginal utility has recently been turned on its head by contemporary economists such as Paul Romer, who we will discuss later.

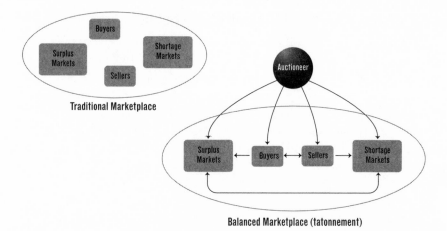

Figure 1.9   While traditional free market models have relied on the ability of buyers and sellers to create efficient markets through the competitive and price dynamics of their interactions, Walras proposed an artificial edifice, which came to be known as the Walrasian Auctioneer, to hover above markets and achieve efficiency by reach "tatonnement"—a state where supply and demand are balanced in order for markets to clear at acceptable prices. Today the Walrasian auctioneer is still the basic concept behind the online exchanges of the X-economy.

themselves must be bidding against each other to shift resources from markets in surplus to those with shortages and assure an efficient use of resources across the economy (Figure 1.9). But how do entire markets bid? Walras used an artifice called an imaginary auctioneer who hovered over the economy and directed underutilized resources from markets where they were unemployed or underemployed to markets where they could command a higher price.

While Walras was speaking figuratively in the 1870s, today one can see how the exchanges we are describing as central constructs of the X-economy are actualizations of the theoretical "Walrasian auctioneer" that economic students have studied for decades—long before the existence of the tools needed to transform Walras' vision into the X-economy.

CHAPTER 2

Rule 1:
The X-Economy
Is Driven by
Demand Chain
Not Supply Chain

"It is not from the benevolence of the butcher, the brewer, or the baker, that we expect our dinner, but from their regard to their own interests. We address ourselves, not to their humanity but to their self love, and never talk to them of our necessities but of their advantages."

Adam Smith

Liquidity

If there is a single concept that best defines the evolution of the X-economy it is that of liquidity. Liquidity, simply stated, is the ability to translate resources into value. The faster the translation occurs, the more liquid a given resource. For example, cash is far more liquid than a piece of real estate, since the former can immediately be transformed into another item of value whereas the latter must undergo a series of intermediate translations before it can be exchanged for another item of value.

This transformation of value as it takes on varying forms is central to the concept of liquidity. To make the discussion more concrete, consider the analogy of a liquid taking the form of its container. No matter what shape the container is, a liquid will easily adapt to its container's most intricate details—in the same way that cash can immediately be translated into any other item of value. But the immediacy of this value translation is contingent on two other factors, market breadth and discount.

> Efficiency seems to provide greater leverage for the buyer while inefficiency tends to favor the seller.

The degree of liquidity requires a context to be measured meaningfully. In other words, if only one buyer and one seller exist, liquidity has no degrees. Increase the number of buyers and the resource being used (cash) is discounted as buyers bid up the price, spending more of the resource for the same amount of a particular good. Increase the number of sellers and the market broadens, decreasing the price of the goods. This is the basic law of supply and demand that we have all grown up with and which Alfred Marshall popularized when he published his *Principles of Economics* in 1890.

However, the law of supply and demand relies on some fundamental inefficiencies and imbalances (Figure 2.1). Some of the best examples are markets such as diamonds and oil, which are controlled by suppliers. Our apologies to those readers who hold fast to the belief that most of the diamonds sold to consumers for jewelry are in fact worth a fraction of the value DeBeers exacts for them through artificial supply controls. This does not mean that there is no inherent value

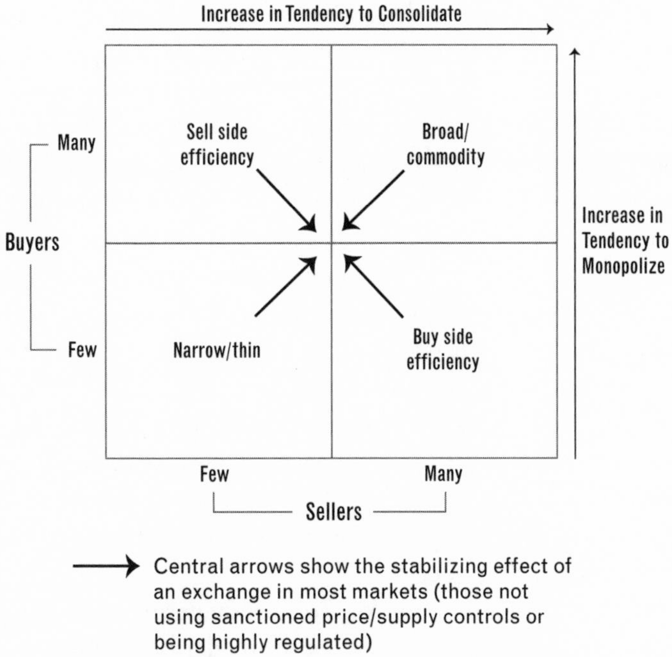
Increase in Tendency to Consolidate
Many
Buyers
Few
Sell side efficiency
Broad/ commodity
Narrow/thin
Buy side efficiency
Increase in Tendency to Monopolize
Few
Many
Sellers
Central arrows show the stabilizing effect of an exchange in most markets (those not using sanctioned price/supply controls or being highly regulated)

Figure 2.1 The many dynamics that shape market efficiency can be summarized as shown in this four quadrant illustration. An exchange will balance these opposing forces to create balanced buy/sell side efficiencies.

in commodities, simply that the value is often manipulated by artificial price controls of inefficient markets.

When a significant dearth of buyers and/or sellers exists, a market is considered to be thin or narrow. Thin markets may result in high discounts or price gouging, require regulation, or simply die off. At the other extreme of this phenomenon are commodity markets, which consist of readily available goods with ample supplies of buyers. Commodity markets tend to be relatively efficient since they are fairly broad.

This leads us to an interesting phenomenon. Efficiency seems to provide greater leverage for the buyer while inefficiency tends to favor the seller. This is the essence of the fear that exchanges engender in most traditional businesses. Namely, if markets get more efficient, then prices will plummet and margins will disappear. Again we can point to the diamond trade which nearly collapsed when word got out after the dissolution of the Soviet Union that Russia was sitting on a stockpile of raw diamonds that would have the same effect on diamond prices that releasing the world's petrochemical reserves would have on the price of gasoline.

So what of that? If it is true and markets are in fact a zero-sum game then won't exchanges drive suppliers out of business, possibly leading to a thin market as suppliers dwindle? In the case of artificially controlled markets where online exchanges can offer alternative channels for procurement, the effect is no less than that of taking away a protected monopoly. Yet, as has been the case with the breakup of some of history's largest monopolies from Standard Oil to AT&T, the resulting component companies have been far more successful despite the turmoil of breaking up.

The reason is that the value of their products and services has been greater when presented to the market in smaller pieces more easily recombined with other pieces of the economy.

And therein lies the power and beauty of liquidity, which adds a new dimension to this equation. To better understand this, let's look at traditional markets as consisting of two axes as show in Figure 2.2. The horizontal axis represents the demand chain and the vertical is the supply chain. But to gain some insight, let's change the labels for just a moment to anonymity (demand chain) and co-opportunity (supply chain). Anonymity reflects the degree to which a supplier understands the market. Co-opportunity represents the degree to which any given enterprise in a value chain can partner with another to produce a new service or product.

Each axis is labeled from 0 to 1, with the value 1 at the center of the X/Y coordinate system. If anonymity is equal to 0, the supplier is completely ignorant of the market and is relying on whim and gut to develop a product that will meet the market's needs. If anonymity is 1, the supplier understands intimately each buyer's requirements. (Note that the scale for anonymity is actually illustrating the degree to which anonymity decreases from left to right.) The same applies to

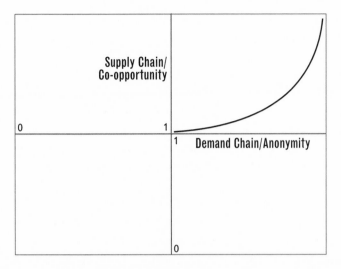

Figure 2.2   The fundamental framework of the X-economy is this simple four quadrant chart that shows how reduced anonymity (demand-side) and increased co-opportunity (supply-side) result in ever expanding opportunities to serve and grow markets.

co-opportunity. If it is equal to 0, the supplier cannot partner with others. As with Henry Ford's early efforts at defining the automobile industry, the supplier wants to control and own every aspect of the raw materials and production. At the other end, 1 indicates that the supplier is partnering to outsource all but core functions.

Given that scenario, you would safely assume that a rating of 1:1 would be the ultimate state of any supply chain. You would be right. But in reaching that conclusion, you have completely ignored the demand chain.

An amazing phenomenon takes place when you move to the upper right quadrant of our matrix—the domain of the X-economy. As exchanges take shape, they initially only serve to accelerate the velocity of transactions. But then they quickly begin to alter the function of market liquidity by introducing a new market dynamic—recombination.

Recombination occurs as exchanges take on the function of matching supply chain to demand chain by tracking the competencies of the supply chain at a low level of granularity while also tracking the preferences and behaviors of the demand chain across discreet buyers and communities. The result is the formation of new products and services to instantly meet the combined requirements of multiple buyers. In practical terms, the exchange now knows intimately the abilities of a large breadth of the supply chain and can map these to the constantly shifting requirements of the market, thus increasing the velocity of innovation, creating constant novelty in products and services (thus maintaining margins), and continuously reforming the supply chain to meet the demand chain.

Now, going one step further, you can envision the liquidity that results from recombination as a third dimension that leaps out from the two-dimensional graph we are using to illustrate supply and demand chain. The effect is to create a third multiplier (demand/supply/liquidity) in the market.

In this upper right-hand quadrant, exchanges become a fundamental construct of the X-economy, with their own set of competencies and communities. These exchanges are what we will later refer to as *vertical portals* or *vortals*. Vortals are highly sophisticated exchanges that create new markets by bringing the supply and demand chains together in novel ways.

This novelty cannot be predicted in the traditional ways that supply chains have reacted to markets. Focus groups, surveys and classic market analysis no longer work. Marketing guru Regis McKenna is fond of saying that even basic staples of the marketer, such as demographic analysis no longer work. We are, according to McKenna, in the age of the "never satisfied" consumer.

It is because of this incredible volatility and inability to form markets around the supply chain that the X-economy is driven by the whim and fancy of the demand chain. Only by keeping pace with the unpredictability of the demand chain can enterprises succeed in the X-economy.

The sort of *recombinant liquidity* we have referred to can be found in a variety of industries (Figure 2.3). One example is the burgeoning market for web developers where one X-economy company, CollabNet, has created what it calls an open-source eBay, referring to the web-based

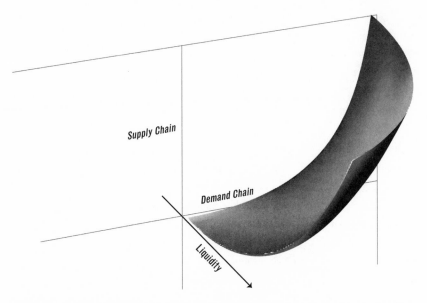

Figure 2.3   By adding a third dimension, liquidity, to our framework we can illustrate the recombinant effect of exchanges on the X-economy, whose growth is now driven by exponential opportunity along three axis rather than two.

consumer auctioneer which has created one of the strongest early brands on the Web.

About 10,000 programmers are members of CollabNet's SourceX-change, which provides an exchange where companies with programming needs post problems that developers then respond to by posting a bid for services. CollabNet then finalizes accepted bids by creating the contracts necessary to perform the engagement.

This sort of instant matching of competency and requirements for services is the essence of the demand-driven processes we are describing. By putting the demand chain in charge innovation is driven to, better yet forced to, higher levels. In the words of CollabNet's vice president of marketing Bernie Mills, "There is an element of spontaneous innovation that happens when you have developers share code and advance that code using open-source principles."

Demand chains are driving markets, making for strange bedfellows among suppliers—and creating bonds of trust where
none would have imagined.

But this increased efficiency is not without its challenges, the foremost of which is the intimacy needed between suppliers and the exchange. Since these suppliers may often compete against each other
there is an obvious reluctance to work with an exchange. And this
brings into play what may be the most important and most often ignored aspect of X-economy companies—trust.

Unfortunately the software revolution in enterprise has focused
developers and users of software systems entirely on transactions. This
transaction infatuation has addressed a relatively small piece of the
trust that ultimately forms the substance of a partner relationship.
Capturing this trust in an exchange and making it part of the community and the economic model may seem nearly impossible. After all, if
it were possible, why hasn't the supply chain done it yet? Therein lies
the answer. The demand chain has not had the clout to make it happen
in all but a few commodity markets due to the supplier leverage in our
lower left-hand quadrant.

Now the tables are turning. Demand chains are driving markets,
making for strange bedfellows among suppliers—and creating bonds
of trust where none would have imagined.

Consider the example of Covisint. How can competitors, who will
remain competitors, justify such an alliance? How can federal regulators
sanction it (which is the case in both the United States and Germany)?
In a word: liquidity. These alliances create value chains that provide for
a payoff measured not only in cost cutting, driving down the average
cost of a purchase order by one order of magnitude, but more importantly, measured in terms of new responsiveness levels of return on innovative capacity. New markets and products take shape much faster,
reducing time to market and increasing returns for all participants.

One way to simplify this is to plot demand chain stimulus against
supply chain responses (Figure 2.4). Demand can come in two forms:
routine (markets ask for products and services that the supply chain

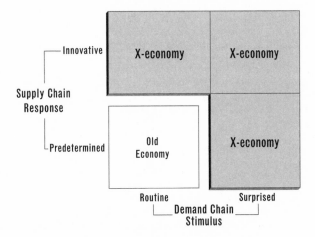

Figure 2.4   X-economy opportunity results from the ability to create liquidity in the three quadrants of the economy that represent innovative supply chain responses and surprise demand chain stimuli.

knows how to produce); and spontaneous (markets ask for products and services that the supply chain has not yet produced). At the same time, the supply chain can respond to both of these stimuli in one of two ways: a predetermined fashion or an innovative fashion. Most old economy models rely on predetermined supply chain responses to routine demand chain stimuli.

Occasionally, however, markets move into one of the other three quadrants of our model. Polaroid's instant camera, Sony's Walkman, Chrysler's minivan are all examples of innovation at work in the upper right-hand quadrant. Each of these products represented a significant departure from the routine stimuli and predetermined responses in their markets.

> The central promise of the X-economy is to make the sort of innovation that has been atypical, typical.

For example, Sony founder Akio Morita had been a vigorous proponent of miniturization for consumer electronics—from the pocket transistor radio to the walkman. Yet despite Sony's very open research and development efforts in both of these products competitors were dumbfounded when each took off beyond anyone's wildest expectations. Consumers were surprised and electronics manufacturers were woefully unprepared to respond when the pocket transistor radio and the walkman were introduced.

In fact, with the first pocket transistor radio, Sony had to order custom shirts for its salespeople with double width breast pockets in which to fit the rather large and cumbersome *pocket* radios. Better financed, more visible competitors could have easily walked away with the market had they not been stuck in their supply chains serving the routing needs of the market.

The lesson here is that radical innovation requires taking radical risks. Ultimately this governs the rate of innovation in any industry.

However, it is not just this sort of radical innovation that is facilitated and accelerated by exchanges. There is constant opportunity for slight refinement of existing products and services in the remaining two quadrants. Product lines are frequently extended to meet routine demand chain stimuli, think for example of how many new cereals come onto the market each year to address the same basic market demand for breakfast in a box. At the same time, existing supply chain deliverables are being repurposed to meet new demand chain stimuli. For instance, how many uses are there, and still climbing, for Arm and Hammer baking soda?

Now consider how exchanges accelerate the ability to address the opportunity latent in the three X-economy quadrants by providing far greater liquidity in the formation of supply chains. The central promise of the X-economy is to make the sort of innovation that has been atypical, typical.

This seems to make sense but it is a business model that needs new metrics to gauge its value as we will see in the remainder of this chapter.

The Value of Liquidity

We are all taught not to repeat the mistakes of the past. History is a vast series of lessons learned and we ignore them at our peril, so we are told. But what if we challenge the generality of that belief? Might it be that, as with so many generalizations, we have lost the essence of truth by using too broad a brush to paint the parable? We are treading on sacred turf here, but we doubt that we are alone.

If a basic tenet of the X-economy is its increased velocity and turbulence, then the past may be the greatest anchor keeping an organization from moving forward to new success and stalling the liquidity of a market. The key to surviving under these conditions is a competency in continuously rebuilding the value chain to drive liquidity through both the demand and supply chains.

Imagine that the X-economy is a whirlpool with items that have fleeting value residing at the vortex, constantly being sucked down and recycled, while items of long-term value, the sort that helps to define the context of our interactions as enterprises and as a society, reside on the periphery, moving rapidly, but remaining intact for a period of time. The question in this model now becomes: Should we use the same benchmark for both of these events, and all of those in-between the two extremes, to govern our actions in the future? Clearly not.

Why do the ranks of the Fortune 500 (even more so their CEOs) change so often? Organizational strength does not come from the knowledge of what has worked in the past, but the ability to regenerate the knowledge of the organization, its processes and its markets. Business assumes a constant vigilance of change, and encourages constant modification, innovation, and liquidity—at ever-increasing rates.

Make no mistake here, every business emphasizes the re-use of previous experiences and practices, but business must also focus on mapping these to the changing landscape of the market. This is where liquidity is created—where supply chain meets demand chain.

If that sounds simple, then try answering the following question: What is your organization's core competency? If you answered with a product name, you're shackled by the past. Chances are, if you answered in this manner, you are referring to your most successful product. Success forms the most restrictive shackles. Your competency must outlive product success. Products should exist at the vortex of the whirlpool—constantly changing. Your core competencies should live at the outer limits of the whirlpool.

Organizational strength does not come from the knowledge of what has worked in the past, but the ability to regenerate the knowledge of the organization, its processes and its markets.

Think of the vortex at the center of this whirlpool as an engine that must constantly be fueled with innovation (Figure 2.5). It does you no good to have core competency if you cannot quickly regenerate ideas and products.

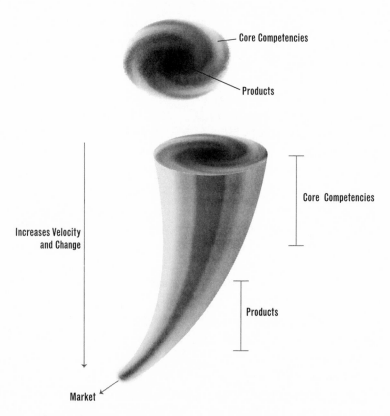

Figure 2.5 Think of an enterprise as a set of core competencies that are constantly driving new products or services. As with a whirlpool, objects on the perimeter move slowly while objects in the vortex are quickly expelled.

Organizations that succeed in the X-economy have reached the stage where their knowledge of the past plays less of a role in guiding their future than does their understanding of current circumstances and an innate ability to create liquidity by processing and responding to these circumstances. The X-economy makes a subtle yet profound shift—from relying on "experience" to relying on "competencies." Knowledge of the past is only valuable inasmuch as it provides a perspective on the future. Competency, on the other hand, equips the organization to respond to as yet unknown forces for change.

The Liquidity Lifecycle

They copied all that they could follow but they couldn't copy my mind, and I left 'em sweating and stealing a year and a half behind.

Rudyard Kipling

But liquidity is not just an abstract concept. It has a very real and tangible existence in the form of products and services. Liquidity also has velocity that can be measured in very concrete terms, as we will see shortly. But, most importantly, liquidity has a lifecycle.

Liquidity is fundamentally the realization of value. Anything of value has a liquidity lifecycle—some very long and some very short. Take a moment and consider that liquidity is like a radioactive isotope—it decays at various rates based on its composition. Some liquidity cycles have a half-life of days, while others will endure for eons. For example, the liquidity lifecycle of popular fashion is clearly short lived. We all laugh at how silly we look in the clothes we thought so stylish in pictures taken just 10 years ago.

On the other hand, the value gained from the great democratic experiments of ancient Athens still applies in our modern day forms of government. Our notion of democracy has a long liquidity lifecycle. It has changed and will continue to change, but it is still based upon and relevant to tenets that emanated from minds many centuries ago.

Our focus here is not on the long-term value systems that provide the framework for an organization but rather the constantly volatile center of the whirlpool we referred to earlier, where innovation must constantly be recirculated.

> Success depends less on the amount of information you have than on the number of connections you can form and reform to link information and people. The dynamic linking aspect of the X-economy enterprise is critical.

As the pace of innovation, mergers and partnerships, and obsolescence increases, the speed of your company's liquidity lifecycle becomes a benchmark challenge for leveraging its intellectual capital into success.

As difficult as it is for those of us who have grown up in the information age to accept, success depends less on the amount of information you have than on the number of connections you can form and reform to link information and people. The dynamic linking aspect of the X-economy enterprise is a critical factor. It is the speed of navigation of these linkages that constitutes liquidity cycles.

Competitive advantage is not only the sum of the intellectual parts of a value chain; it is the *speed of summation*. The liquidity cycle provides a measure of an organization's or a value chain's competitive advantage.

There are four steps in the liquidity lifecycle that determine competitive advantage, they are:

1. Supply chain awareness
2. Supply chain responsiveness
3. Demand chain responsiveness
4. Demand chain awareness

The liquidity lifecycle is a series of interactions that constitute a market's (supply and demand side) ability to realize liquidity (Figure 2.6).

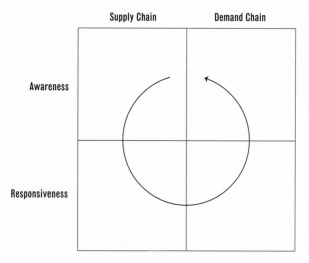

Figure 2.6   The four quadrants of the liquidity lifecycle represent the series of interactions that constitute a market's ability to realize liquidity. The shorter the time to traverse the path shown by the counter clockwise arrow, the higher the liquidity—or what we will call *Return on Time.*

It's important to keep in mind that, for our purposes, and in the context of the X-economy, the term organization and the collective of organizations that make up a specific instance of the supply chain are synonymous.

Supply Chain Awareness

In its simplest terms, supply chain awareness is the ability of an organization to quickly assess its inventory of skills and core competencies. This appears to be a simple task, yet few organizations have mastered it. Consider, for example, what the core competency of your organization is. Ask yourself, "Why are we successful?" Again, savvy players will not respond with a product name, recognizing that this is not a competency but a temporary market advantage or commodity. In today's market products must be continuously reinvented, with an ever-decreasing product lifecycle. It is what Peter Drucker refers to as *organized abandonment,* the ability to literally cannibalize your greatest successes in order to deliver the next successful product before your competitors.

> Organizations with a rigid functional structure most often define their core competency as their products and services, not their skills.

The X-economy enterprise thinks of supply chain awareness in terms of "What do we do?" as opposed to "What do we make?" For example, an architect's job can be described as either to design buildings or to translate human needs into aesthetically pleasing and functionally responsive structures. It's a lot easier to say that a residential architect designs ranches or split-levels. But what happens to the architect if demand for these types of buildings declines, or even disappears? Competencies always outlive products.

Strong emphasis on functional organization structures that often permeate traditional companies inhibits the development of supply chain awareness. Organizations with a rigid functional structure most often define their core competency as their products and services, not their skills. As James Brian Quinn recounts in *The Intelligent Enterprise*,[1] "The question usually posed is, 'How can we position our products (or product lines) for competitive advantage?' not, 'What critical skills should we develop to be best in the world from our customers' viewpoint?' The former builds current profits, the latter builds long-term preeminence."

It is this long-term preeminence that organizations need most if they are to weather changing markets. But the systems and institutions in place in many organizations undermine this objective. This is especially true in functional organization structures where, as Quinn notes, "each functional group has a psychological and political need to see itself as the company's special source of strategic strength. In

---

[1] James Brian Quinn, "The Intelligent Enterprise" (New York: Free Press, 1992).

neither event are there strong incentives to build the cross-divisional corporate skills that would lead to enterprise preeminence. Corporate effectiveness is undercut to satisfy personal or divisional goals."

Vortals not only offer incentives for building cross-industry skill sets, they also make the collective supply chain aware of these skills, thereby creating high levels of supply chain awareness. Creating this level of awareness is indeed the principle challenge in the X-economy. Once a supply chain has established its own awareness it can proceed through the remainder of the liquidity cycle. Until then it is relying far more on the temporal success of its products than on its core skills and competencies.

Supply Chain Responsiveness

The awareness of a supply chain's competencies does not guarantee a clear path to successful products or services. A supply chain may be well aware of its strengths and market demand, yet not be able to adequately effect change within itself quickly enough to meet market requirements.

Supply chain responsiveness considers how quickly the collective competencies of a supply chain can be translated into actions to bring a product to market or respond to a customer need. It's the ability to respond quickly and seize an opportunity in spite of the existing rigidity of a value chain or the lack of existing cooperation between the right set of partners.

Demand Chain Responsiveness

In any organization or industry, success is ultimately measured by the ability to best meet the requirements of this step in the liquidity cycle. Ultimately, success is measured by the ability to respond to turbulence in a market by making decisions without having to coordinate and consider all of the factors in a complex business and market environment. Demand chain responsiveness is that ability to "turn on a dime" when the crosshairs of the supply chain align with the requirements of the demand chain. This is the essence of competitive advantage—a

level of responsiveness to environmental conditions that is significantly faster than that of competitors.

Demand Chain Awareness

There's no point in responding quickly, though, if it's too late. Like a
numbed hand placed on a hot stove, some companies may only become aware of the extent of their lack of awareness after they smell
their own burning flesh.

Organizations who succeed in the X-economy, on the other hand,
are "wired" with high levels of continuous awareness (both demand
chain and supply chain). Demand chain awareness represents the organization's ability to understand how the market perceives the value associated with its products and services. It also means the cognizance of
market trends, competitive actions, government regulations, and any
other relevant market forces that exist outside of the organization itself.
When coupled with supply chain awareness, demand chain awareness
leads to the formation of entirely new markets.

This is one of the cornerstones of the Internet where new business
models are sprouting up at an unprecedented pace. The velocity of the
Internet provides an incredible opportunity to act on the market's reaction to new products. However, new models for capturing market
response is just as critical. For example, the ability to capture buying
trends of buyers and then use these to suggest products or services that
address similar needs is the very essence of demand chain awareness.

It is important to realize that demand chain awareness is more
than just a function of extensive focus groups and market research.
These can often provide false clues. They provide testimony to what
the market needs today, or yesterday, rather than what it will need in
the future. In the worst case, they provide only the answers that the
demand chain thinks the supply chain wants to hear. A classic example is that of New Coke, which, despite heavy market analysis, proved
the ultimate folly of focus groups. The reality is that as markets move
at an ever-faster pace, market research is reaching the end of its
useful lifecycle. You simply cannot research a market that has not yet

experienced a product or service, and often can't tell you what it thinks it will need in the future.

Demand chain driven companies such as Dell and Cisco Systems do not rely on focus groups to shape market direction but connect directly with the customer by allowing their products to be "built" online. By putting product configuration software in hands of customers through their Web sites, they have literally joined the supply chain with the demand chain.

How Organizations Demonstrate the Liquidity Lifecycle

To make the picture of the liquidity lifecycle clearer, let's examine how different organizations behave in the various stages. Our earlier illustration showed the liquidity lifecycle as a matrix of four cells, corresponding to the evolution of innovation. For organizations that are not liquidity-driven, the cells of the liquidity lifecycle look like Figure 2.7.

	Supply Chain	*Demand Chain*
Awareness	Rigid value chains, lack of knowledge sharing among partners, static policies and procedures for transactions, lack of an awareness as to core competencies.	Delayed customer feedback loops result from belabored market research and a reliance only on product branding.
Responsiveness	New ideas are stifled by a hierarchical command and control structure in the value chain. Vertical integration of supply chain makes partnering difficult.	Slow distribution channels result in standardized products, long duration's between innovation cycles, and extensive emphasis on supply chain rate of return.

Figure 2.7   Liquidity lifecycle.

	Supply Chain	*Demand Chain*
Awareness	Always collectively aware of strengths and weaknesses across the constituents of a supply chain or industry.	Constantly removing filters between the market and its innovative capacity to form true partnerships with prospects and customers. Relying on recombination of the demand and supply chain in order to create new markets.
Responsiveness	Able to instantly organize skills and partners based on an unfiltered assessment of supply chain resources and demand chain market demands/ opportunities.	The final measure of liquidity as a perpetual ability to meet the market on its own terms— even when the market cannot articulate these and a clear return is not present.

Figure 2.8   Lifecycle for leveraged knowledge.

In organizations that are liquidity driven, all four cells of the liquidity cycle are permeable, allowing fast partnering and the immediate transfer of competencies, knowledge, and services among partners in and between the cells.

Organizations that leverage knowledge have characteristics in the cells that look like Figure 2.8. Liquidity is measured by the speed with which an organization flows through these four links. This represents an organization's return on time.

Return on Time

Return on time (ROT) measures an organization's ability to sustain innovation over a period of time. The higher the ROT, the more innovative and competitive the organization is and the more likely it is to be applying the principles of a strong liquidity cycle.

The value of an organization's return on time can be described quantitatively and looks like this:

$$ROT = \frac{Percent\ of\ profit}{100} \times \frac{Sustained\ years}{Number\ of\ years}$$

As an example, a company that for the past 5 years has derived 50 percent of its profit for each year from products that have been introduced in that same year has an ROT of 2.5. Not bad. However, a company that for 10 years has derived 100 percent of its yearly profit from product introduced in the last 3 years would have an ROT of 3.3. Even better. Table 2.1 provides some basic examples:

A complete ROT analysis must look at the lifecycle and contribution of every product over the time period being measured, including the complexity of multiple product lines and varying profit contributions by each line.

However, even a simple analysis of available public data provides a clear sense for where your organization stands in its industry relative to its competitors. For example, consider if you are in the high-technology market for integrated circuitry, at least 80 percent of your profit must come from products introduced in the last 24 months. If not, you are out of business.

The last thing to keep in mind about ROT is that it is a relative measure. There is no absolute. As with any other measure of return (return on investment, internal rate of return, return on assets, etc.) you need only do better than your competitors in your market's context to be successful.

Table 2.1   Examples of Return on Time

ROT	Percent Profit	Number of Years	Sustained Years
2.5	50	1	5
3.3	100	3	10
2.3	70	3	10
1.0	100	20	20

Demand-Side Economics

While ROT provides one simple method to benchmark an organization's ability to generate liquidity, it does not consider the dynamics of an exchange that involves multiple organizations.

As business and financial analysts alike seek to quantify the value of X-economy business models, considerable attention is given to the lifetime value of a customer. In other words, once a customer has been successfully secured for the first time, what amount of business will he or she provide over the course of the relationship?

At the root of this question is the notion that the cost of obtaining a new customer is greater than the cost of retaining one. As a result, any business with an existing customer base has an apparent cost (and time) advantage over a competitor without. As such, businesses are driven to lock-in customers with economic incentives such as discounts for repeat business, as well as proprietary approaches which increase the cost of switching to competing alternatives, called switching costs.

A popular example of switching costs is attributed to the story of the QWERTY keyboard layout. Invented by Christopher Sholes and introduced by gun manufacturer E. Remington & Sons with the Type Writer, an eponymous product whose proprietary brand name evolved into a standard of its own, the QWERTY layout was designed not for its superiority but rather its *inferiority*—specifically to slow-down typing speeds in order to prevent jamming by the Type Writer's clunky nineteenth-century mechanics. Today known as the Universal format, the QWERTY layout has survived all would-be competitors, including the much-lauded Dvorak design, widely held as superior in both typing speed and user ergonomics.

Given the relatively slow pace that the average computer user types today, the prospect of a marginal increase in speed or comfort fails to counter the increased cost and effort required to re-learn a new keyboard layout. Thus, in a contemporary context, the switching costs inherent in the Dvorak design eliminate it as a serious contender to the Universal layout. During the middle of the last century, however, this was not necessarily the case. The economic benefit of increased typing productivity would have in many cases outweighed the cost of mechanical conversion and personnel retraining needed for the Dvorak design, according to the claims by Dvorak himself and other proponents of the design. If so, why did the Universal design triumph?

The enduring success of the Universal layout in the face of seemingly superior competition flies in the face of neoclassical economic theory, and indeed is often held up by economists as an example of market failure. To the contrary, however, it is an example of rational market behavior in the context of "increasing returns," an economic theory popularized by Paul M. Romer, professor of economics in the Graduate School of Business at Stanford University and a senior fellow of the Hoover Institution. (Contrast this with the Walrasian theory of marginal utility in Chapter 1.)

Increasing returns presents a lock-in scenario where switching costs are magnified beyond what is encountered in a discrete transaction and rather are a function of community behavior as a whole. It is important to appreciate, however, that this is driven by the demand chain, and not a phenomenon of monopolistic coercion. Only the market can create lock-in, by rallying around a preferred approach or product. But markets are stochcastic rather than deterministic in their behavior, and as such are shaped by many different externalities other than pure empirical data. These often random events reflect the changing circumstances that frame buyer behavior at specific points in time and may be otherwise indifferent to design superiority.

In the case of the Universal keyboard layout, it at first persevered only marginally as the most common "standard" in a time of competing alternatives, and for decades remained one of many choices. What tipped the market in its favor was a series of seemingly serendipitous events, rather than predatory marketing practices, which eventually lead to virtual absolute dominance. In a process often referred to as *path dominance*, circumstances such as the availability of training courses and standardization by the U.S. military led to a greater familiarity with the Universal layout and, in the interest of skills portability, a tacit preference to the design. By the second half of the twentieth century, the compound impact of these events meant that typists were far more likely to have trained on this format and were unlikely to switch without significant economic incentive—clearly more than was offered by the Dvorak design.

This geometric progression is characteristic of the increasing returns dynamic. The adoption of standard practices and products evolve in a nearly linear progression until hitting an inflection point where demand starts to move exponentially. In the case of the Universal layout, it took nearly a century for this effect to set in. In the case of the fax machine, it took even longer. Patented in 1843 by Scottish inventor Alexander Bain, then promoted commercially by AT&T in 1925, the fax machine never moved beyond the experimental phase until Sharp introduced a mass market product in 1984, when 80,000 units were sold. From that point it took the entire market three years to sell one million units (in 1987) then in the following year two million units were sold. By 1990, the presence of a fax machine in the office environment was nearly as commonplace as the telephone. This interval from introduction to adoption is the cycle called *time-to-community* introduced in Chapter 1.

The exponential growth of the fax machine was not driven simply by a reduction in cost, rather increased affordability was ultimately a result of the rapid rise in demand. The compound growth of demand illustrates an aspect of increasing returns theory called the *effect of network externalities,* which leads to the increasing economic value of a product or practice as usage grows. This creates a positive feedback loop where growth in popularity leads to increased use that leads to greater demand. Through this effect the opposite also applies—decreased usage leads to corresponding reduction in value. As a result of this effect, the dynamics of increasing returns presents a scenario of "winner takes most" where one approach locks-in market dominance and the "losers" are left to fight over the remaining crumbs or transition to another market segment that offers greater chance for success. As a result, time-to-community becomes a proxy for economic success—the first to reach community is the clear successor (for as long as they can keep it).

As we have shown, increasing returns is not a phenomenon unique to the X-economy. What is indeed new, however, and prescient to any examination of the opportunities offered by the X-economy is the compression of the time-to-community cycle. In an environment where customers and competition remain just a click away, the ability to organize the elements of community are accessible at unprecedented levels. One of the most notable examples of this is Napster, who with little marketing or commercial infrastructure grew to a community of 50 million users in little more than a year, dwarfing competing approaches by a factor of more than 10 to 1 and turning the recording industry on its head in the process.

The dynamics of increasing returns presents a scenario of "winner takes most" where one approach locks-in market dominance and the "losers" are left to fight over the remaining crumbs or transition to another market segment that offers greater chance for success. As a result, time-to-community becomes a proxy for economic success.

Despite the opportunities presented by the increasing returns dynamic, many early e-business models failed to leverage the power of community. Little more than new wine in old bottles, they share a mass-market perspective where each new buyer will likely result in one new sale. This is at the root of any strategy focusing on the promotion of only one business or product type, and where sales growth is a function of replenishment and new customer acquisition. Whether or not explicit in their design, this is an inevitable limitation of any e-business initiative built around the notion of simply replicating old economy sales and distribution models in an online context. While the opportunity of these business models may seem promising in the face of the worldwide market offered by the Web, the value proposition is still linear, and by comparison myopic. Think of this equation as "n to 1" where the aggregate value of commercial activity is based on the number of buyers. As we will illustrate, these models fail to capture the benefit of increasing returns.

Metcalfe's Law: The Compound Benefit of Communities

To understand how increasing returns applies to the X-economy model of communities, imagine an "$n \times n$" matrix where each participant is positioned to benefit from the other. At play here is the increasing returns effect of networks, popularly known as *Metcalfe's Law*. Simply put, the law dictates that the value of a network is equal to the square of its members ($v = n \times n$; where n is the number of network participants and v is cumulative value of the network). First articulated by George Gilder on behalf of Bob Metcalfe, originator of the dominant local area network protocol called Ethernet, the law was originally devised to explain the compounding qualities of electronic networks. The same math, however, is involved in the formation of N:N communities, and as such it is a fundamental metric of the X-economy.

To appreciate the differences here, first picture two linear value chains pointed end-to-end. One is the supply chain focused on bringing a product to market. The other is the demand chain, driving the purchase of a product. The point at which they meet is the consummation of a sale—the transaction. Each of the activities leading up to the transaction are all linked by the common interest of enabling the sale. They are part of a virtual community, however, they may have no awareness or visibility of each other. There is no coordination outside of the discrete handoffs from one activity to another. For most organizations, this is illustrative of the way their value chains are organized.

For the N:N community, picture a connected matrix of participants joined by the common goal of commercial success. The degree of value creation is directly related to the level of connectivity between community members. Rather than the command-and-control environment that define traditional, vertically integrated value chains, the N:N community presents an opportunity for sense-and-respond agility. In this context, value chains are assembled based on the best set of components for each new opportunity, and then disassemble just as quickly.

The speed and ease with which this is executed is the measure of the community's liquidity. As we discussed in the section on the *liquidity lifecycle,* value creation depends less on proprietary information and much more on the speed with which connections can be formed.

To calculate the potential of N:N communities in accordance with Metcalfe's Law, first consider the traditional commercial model where a group of 10 organizations serviced by 10 competing sellers would likely represent 10 possible transactions (1:1) (Figure 2.9). To the community model of an N:N community, however, this may represent 10 × 10 or 100 possible transactions. Thus doubling the number of buyers and sellers to 20 will likely mean a total of 20 transactions for the old model, and as such the market grows in an arithmetic or linear progression. Within the N:N model, however, it results in 20 × 20 or 400 possible transactions. This quickly adds up. If the two models grew at the same rate (doubled-annually) for 10 years, the difference is a matter of 512,000 percent (see Figure 2.10).

Quadratic Capacity

Possibilities do not add up. They multiply.

Paul Romer

As promising as this model appears, the astute reader may be skeptical about the possibility of ever realizing these quantum gains. Indeed, there is a school of thought that dictates that the theoretical potential

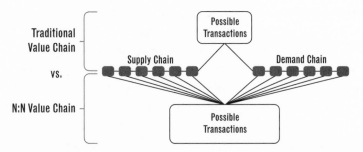

Figure 2.9   N:N value chains support connections and visibility among all community members. Traditional value chains offer visibility only to the tail ends of the supply and demand chains.

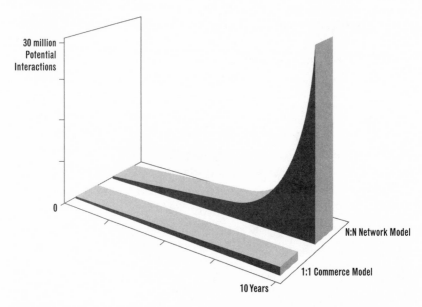

Figure 2.10   The N:N network model enables exponential growth of community interactions. This growth reflects the increasing returns dynamics generated by N:N communities.

of a network is never realized, as network friction grows in parallel with the geometric progression of the network. As a result, only a fraction of potential capacity is ever reached. This concept, called *quadratic capacity*, is often applied to physical networks such as telephone systems and the Internet, with the intent of illustrating that their actual realizable value grows in a linear progression, even though the potential combination of connections grow exponentially. For example, while most U.S. households are connected to the global telephone network only a fraction of potential users can access the system at any given time. (Most everyone has received this message at one time or another, "All circuits are busy. Please try your call again later.")

Quadratic capacity further dictates that as a network grows and interdependent entities grow, so does the likelihood of failure. Proponents of this notion have devised a simple formula to demonstrate the inverse rate of reliability with network growth:

$$1 - (1 - p)^n$$

where n equals the number of nodes on the network and p equals the probability of a failure in a single node. According to this theorem, if a computer has a 3 percent probability of failure on its own, a network of only a dozen of the same computers would be more than 10 times as likely to fail.

There is a school of thought that dictates that the theoretical potential of a network is never realized, as network friction grows in a parallel with the geometric progression of the network.

Do the same sobering laws of governance hold back the potential of Metcalfe's Law as it applies X-economy communities? Some critics would argue it does. This argument is often rooted in Malthusian thinking, a popular reference for the upward limits of economic growth. Thomas Robert Malthus published *An Essay on the Principle of Population* in 1798 to explain the effect of population growth as it relates to the ability of the world's resources to sustain it. Simply put, human population increases in the same geometric rate as presented by Metcalfe's Law, however subsistence increases in a linear progression. As such, if left unchecked, mankind will quickly outgrow its ability to sustain itself and starve as a result. Thus, network growth is bound by a finite ability to utilize its potential capacity, the capacity for sustained economic growth is limited by finite resources.

Malthus' theory has formed the basis of many arguments favoring the imposition of explicit economic growth restrictions and population control. One of these was Paul Erhlich and his book *The Population Bomb,* in which he predicted we would by now be facing worldwide famine and widespread disease. Erhlich was far from alone when he first promoted his ideas in the late 1960s, because the notion of diminishing returns has for decades reflected mainstream economic thinking.

To illustrate this line of reasoning, consider the notion of economic equilibrium—the point at which buyers' demand for a particular product and the ability of the market to supply it are in balance. Simply put, the market price is set by both the cost of producing a product and the amount buyers are willing to pay. Although the market's ability to supply the product may increase if buyers raise the price they are willing to pay, aggregate demand is likely to decrease at the higher price point. As Malthusian thinking dictates, the ability to supply the market with finite resources decreases as they are consumed and as such the cost of producing more of the same resource increases. The seller's dilemma is a choice of selling less of the product at a higher price point or reducing profit margins by maintaining the same price.

In either case, the outcome presents a scenario of diminishing returns to the seller, eventually leading to their abandonment of the market or the collapse of the competitive landscape into a limited number of sellers. It is in this context that economists such as R. H. Coase step in. Coase postulated that transaction cost economics illustrates how vertically integrated value chains shape market dominance, by pointing to relative size as a leading determinant of competitive advantage. Coase's work explains how relatively fixed transaction costs eventually drive all mature markets into stagnating oligopolies, where only a handful of sellers are able to maintain economy of scale and profits in the face of diminishing returns, inevitably forcing out price competition and, as result, innovation.

Applied to traditional models of online marketplaces, Malthusian thinking illustrates the finite limitations of growth potential. For example, an insurance underwriter may only offer a marginal economic incentive in exchange for access to a larger pool of customers. Suppliers will provide discounts in exchange for large sales volumes, but this too has its limits. In this context, the ability for demand aggregation enabled by the marketplace presents a zero sum game where the discount to the buyer will only be as great as the degree to which the seller's cost of sales is reduced (minus the transaction fee charged by the exchange).

Sellers are bound by limits of cost and resources, and as such are able to offer only a finite degree of economic incentive to generate new demand. Thus the 1:1 and N:1 market models growth is inherently limited by existing demand.

While the linear value proposition of traditional market models is subject to diminishing returns, what Malthus and his proponents have failed to consider is the synergy generated by N:N communities. Rather than competing over finite resources and static buyer demand, the N:N community model enables the development of new opportunities maximizing each aspect of the value chain. This notion is a function of the same theories of increasing returns and economic growth developed by Romer. As Romer points out, the molecular decomposition of otherwise vertically integrated value chains allows for the creation of economic value where linear aggregation alone would not. By maximizing the value of each individual component, through a variety of new combinations, organizations are able to take advantage of an increasing array of activities. As Romer explains,

> Every generation has perceived the limits to growth that finite resources and undesirable side effects would pose if no new recipes or ideas were discovered. And every generation has underestimated the potential for finding new recipes and ideas. We consistently fail to grasp how many ideas remain to be discovered. The difficulty is the same one we have with compounding. Possibilities do not add up. They multiply.[2]

Romer turns the propositions of both Malthus and Coase upside down by illustrating the greatest source of value creation comes not from squeezing the last drops out of the ever-decreasing resources of market, but through the discovery of new market opportunities and economies of scale.

---

[2] Paul Romer, "Increasing Returns and New Developments in the Theory of Growth," Working Paper No. 3098, National Bureau of Economic Research, September 1989.

Consider five organizations with opportunities in business areas outside of their usual level of risk tolerance and expected rate of return. Traditionally they would be faced with the choice of accepting business under less than desirable conditions or turning away the opportunity. Now examine this in the context of the N:N market community.

Consider, again, the role of an insurance underwriter. If each of these five businesses were to approach an insurer separately, the cost of insurance may be forbiddingly high. By spreading the risk, however, the insurer is able to offer a more palatable rate without sacrificing their own margins. The insurer is able to aggregate these policies for sale to the aftermarket, and the five policy buyers are able to further increase what had been unattractively low margins.

In the X-economy, N:N communities support the decomposition of value chains into basic molecular elements to be reassembled into virtually unlimited combinations of value creating entities.

Add to the equation a net increase in margins through a reduction in cost of goods sold by taking advantage of the manufacturers' excess plant capacity. Add to this the ability to collaboratively source raw materials, enabling both the supplier and buyers to reduce costs through a production run.

Factor into this the ability for each of the five to work with other community members to find surplus capacity on shipping routes, enabling an economy of scale in distribution where all participants see a net increase in productivity. Add to this the saving in coordination efforts by using the collaborative logistics tools of the community.

Each of the five further reduce the risk involved in each of these transactions by utilizing escrow services, letters of credit, and other transaction management services available to the community.

The result of this example is 25 individual transactions through the N:N community where otherwise there would be none, illustrating how the dynamics of Metcalfe's Law play out in an environment where all members of the community have visibility and connectivity. It also demonstrates the source of value creation from decomposing value chain components into molecular elements. In each case, the participants were able to derive value from resources otherwise locked-up in vertically integrated value chains.

In the X-economy, the value of a community is directly proportional to the degree of connectivity between community members. The ability to access surplus production capacity and the other activities we have described is not a new phenomenon. What is new and unique to the N:N community model, however, is the efficiency with which the resources can be identified and coordinated. The result is the ability to profitably exploit opportunities otherwise not economically viable.

In the vertically integrated world of the old economy, the few dominant players at the top of oligopolist markets use economies of scale to force out new entrants and competition. Here size is a deterrent to market entry, where existing value chains are shaped into a virtually impenetrable fortress. Inside these walls, however, is a reality of diminishing returns and stagnating innovation. In the X-economy, N:N communities support the decomposition of value chains into basic molecular elements to be reassembled into virtually unlimited combinations of value-creating entities.

As with any molecular activity, however, these formations do not spontaneously assemble. An environment must be in place that supports the growth and creation of the community. These environments represent a new breed of community-based business models discussed in Chapter 3.

Takeaways

This chapter has focused on liquidity, or the ability to translate a resource into value, and its impact on businesses. The faster this resource can be translated into value, the greater that resource's liquidity.

Liquidity has a measurable velocity as well as a lifecycle, described in four steps that will determine the uniqueness and longevity of an organization as well as its ability to create innovation and survive change based on its evolution within these four categories. They are:

- *Supply chain awareness.* Ability of an organization to quickly assess its inventory of skills and core competencies.
- *Supply chain responsiveness.* Ability to quickly rally the collective competencies of a supply chain in order to bring a product to market or respond to a customer need.
- *Demand chain responsiveness.* Ability to respond to changes in a complex market by rapidly making decisions and taking action to align supply chain capabilities with the requirements of the demand chain.
- *Demand chain awareness.* Ability to understand how the market perceives the value associated with its products and services, and to recognize and decipher market trends and other factors that potentially impact the business offerings or customer needs.

The value of return-on-time measures an organization's ability to sustain innovation over a period of time. The higher the ROT, the more innovative and competitive the organization is and the more likely it is to be applying the principles of a strong liquidity cycle.

Businesses in the X-economy are able to maximize their return on time and increase their resource liquidity in a way described by Metcalfe's Law: *The value of a network is equal to the square of its members*—whether computers, phones, or value chain participants. The X-economy provides the opportunity to create these N:N communities by linking any number of value chain participants, vastly increasing the number of potential relationships and, with it, the potential number of interactions and transactions. When a community has reached critical mass, the dynamic of increasing returns perpetuates its success through the effect of positive feedback loops that increase the value of the community as a whole with the introduction of each new member.

CHAPTER 3

Rule 2:
The X-Economy
Is a Community,
Not a Market

The Emergence of the Exchange

It is well known what a middleman is: he is a man who bamboozles one party and plunders the other.
Benjamin Deisraeli

Metcalfe's Law describes not only the way markets behave but also points to the incredible challenge involved in trying to create efficient mechanisms for forming communities. The necessity to manage the "many-to-many" commercial relationships that define these complex markets is an incredible burden that stalls the ability of any supply chain to transform itself when a new opportunity, product, or service comes along. For example, in industries such as plastics and metals, each segment may be comprised of thousands of suppliers who deal with thousands of processors and refiners who deal with thousands of different grades of materials. The result is literally trillions of possible combinations.

Addressing the fragmentation of markets such as these requires the role of a neutral intermediary, bound to neither buyer nor seller, capable of facilitating direct exchanges between any two parties in a transaction.

A new class of upstarts is doing precisely this, smashing traditional notions of intermediated channels and dramatically shifting the balance of power within the distribution arena. Rather than operating as product sellers, these new businesses are true market makers, building NASDAQ-like exchanges to unlock new levels of liquidity and redefining trading routes. Utilizing dynamic pricing and trading capabilities within the context of the Web, they connect a matrix of buyers and sellers in relationships where they are at the center of the value chain.

The most visible difference with the exchange business model is the presence of a dynamic trading floor. The introduction of auctions to commerce is nothing new, in fact exchanges have existed in the offline world since the origins of commerce. What is revolutionary about online auctions is their application to segments of industry that have been otherwise immune to dynamic trading practices, such as demand-driven pricing and fluid supplier sourcing. Industries such as steel, petrochemical, and auto manufacturing that had long been defined by Byzantine layers of vertically integrated bureaucracy, have been the earliest adopters of the exchange model. While not every product or service will be sold through an auction, exchanges are redefining thousands of distribution channels and trading communities that have over decades, in some cases centuries, become congested by oligopolists and stodgy business practices.

The most dynamic exchange model is that which most directly parallels the NASDAQ type of electronic exchange—the many-to-many model also known as the *bidirectional exchange.* The manner in which the NASDAQ network of securities brokers operates—by hosting two forms of market marker or intermediary, one representing an interested buying party and one representing selling party—is an example of this form of exchange. When casual investors look at activity across the NASDAQ market they are typically looking at a Level 1 screen showing quoted stock prices. Implicit in this is the fact that two interested parties were connected, but specifics of this are hidden.

When brokers and traders subscribing to the NASDAQ network look at the market, they also see the Level 2 screen which is split into two sides, one showing buy orders and the other sell orders by other market makers across the network.

The ability to assess supply and demand for a stock allows traders to profit from the spread of the two orders, matching a seller with a lower price requirement to a buyer with a higher one. As a function of this, prices will fluctuate up or down within the bilateral exchange, but only move in one direction with other auction models (down for reverse, up for forward model). This dynamic greatly increases the volatility of the market by laying all the cards on the table. Rather than playing a game of poker where traders have to guess at what the other is holding, the Level 2 screen allows them to view the entire spectrum of buying and selling interests and to adjust orders accordingly. Played out across a network of 500,000 traders, the result is a fast-paced, dynamic market with considerable volume and liquidity. Looking at the NASDAQ of today compared with the NYSE of 20 years ago is a great proxy for where exchange trading practices and the X-economy are headed.

Figure 3.1 is an example of the bidirectional exchange, as seen by the buyer. In this case, the Seattle Mariners are using the auction services of *@themoment,* an example of the Business Service Provider discussed later in this chapter, to offer live trading of game tickets. The buyer is able to monitor market behavior in real-time, including the ratio of bids to the seller's asking price, called the spread in the Pitometer window in the upper right-hand corner of the screen. Although buyers do not have direct access to specific bids, the monitor shows the relation of bids (indicated by the orbiting dots) to the buyers desired asking price (center dot).

Exchanges with a bidirectional bid/ask capability behave in exactly the same way as the NASDAQ. Unlike the other models we will describe, where prices and other criteria are displayed publicly, the market makers in the bidirectional exchange mask this information from both buying and selling parties. This is where the intermediaries come in. Just as with the NASDAQ, these exchanges literally have traders who subscribe to the network and stare at the screen of market makers. These human intermediaries are necessary for price normalization by

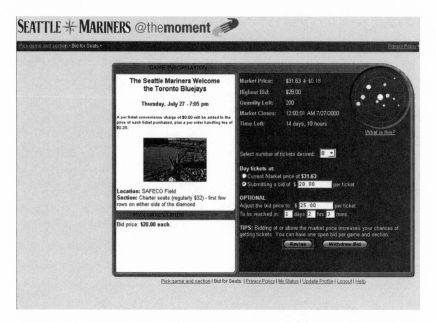

Figure 3.1   Exchange interfaces must provide visibility of basic trading parameters such as price and availability. More sophisticated environments, such as @theMoment shown here, will also show bidding activity.

bridging the information gap in markets without absolute standardization. A share of IBM is a share of IBM, but an electrical component from an anonymous source requires human intervention in the form of inspection and verification in order to demand a competitive market price.

This type of anonymity is a key criterion to maintaining price stability on the highly volatile markets these exchanges operate in. For example, NECX, an electronic components exchange now owned by VerticalNet, provides market-making services to companies such as large buyers and manufacturers of semiconductors and microchips. The market for these commodities is particularly sensitive to the balance of supply and demand. If a manufacturer or a buyer of a particular component finds itself with a surplus, trying to wholesale the lot on their own would inevitably disrupt the balance of supply and demand and result in an immediate price drop across the board. This clearly would negatively impact other transactions in progress or other contract purchases with fixed price points.

By anonymously liquidating these components through the exchange, the seller may receive less revenue than was initially expected for the lot, but it does not otherwise disrupt their business model. Similarly, a buyer with an unexpected need to purchase components wishes to do so without tipping his hand to the rest of the selling community, thereby unnecessarily driving up the price. For this reason, two critical functions these exchanges serve is both in making markets by bringing together buyers and sellers, as well as maintaining anonymity from the point of taking over inventory through to the settlement of the transaction. At every step, the exchange facilitates the trade without the buyer or seller ever learning the other's identity. It is important to note, however, that this is not an entirely automated or mechanized process. There are several points during the negotiation and fulfillment process where a human intermediary is necessary, notably for the inspection and distribution of purchased goods when tangible products are involved (e.g., the purchase of fish rather than intangibles such as bandwidth or electricity). Yet to both the buyer and seller, this is a closed-door process.

It should be clear from this description that the bidirectional exchange facilitates trades that are not purely direct between buyer and seller, but are done with a high level of intermediation. The dynamics of this model are such that the market maker assumes liability, of which it is not free until after the trade has been settled. For this reason, these exchanges must highly scrutinize the participants they allow, as well as focus only on highly commoditized markets. One of the best examples of this are the markets that are coming out of the deregulation of utilities for trading commodities such as electricity and water. Here the commodity traded may not move physically from one party to another, but rather what is traded are the rights of use. For this reason, the prequalification of trading partners and the integrity of the settlement process is critical to these exchanges.

A good example is Altra Energy, a large business-to-business exchange for wholesale energy, including electric, natural gas, and natural gas liquids, that helps its members identify, trade, and manage the many transactions that occur daily in these markets. The Altra Energy exchange is managing over 12,000 transactions a month, on average, that represent 2,200 individual buyers and sellers at 500 of the largest energy companies. As part of the services it offers to its customers, Altra utilizes two types of prequalification processes as a method for guaranteeing the viability of its trading partner members and the transactions conducted through the exchange.

For the electric power market, the buyers and sellers prequalify each other, using assistance from Altra to develop business rules specific to each trading partner which will then be used by the exchange software to identify and complete transactions. Transactions are kept within the limits and boundaries of those rules, helping ensure the legitimacy of the transaction and minimizing business risk. The identities of the buyer and seller are kept anonymous until after the transaction is consummated, at which point the identities are revealed to the parties in the transaction. Settlement of the transaction occurs between the buyer and seller, and any dispute that arises from nonpayment or failure to deliver must be resolved between the transacting parties.

In the case of natural gas, however, Altra Energy goes one step further. When a new gas customer joins the exchange, Altra does a complete credit check on the new member. This evaluation information is then provided to Altra's insurance provider, who writes a default policy for a specific amount on the new member. This policy becomes, in effect, the customer's line of credit within the exchange. When this customer enters into a purchase transaction through the exchange, delivery of the gas is made into an Altra account on a specified pipeline on the scheduled delivery date. As soon as Altra has taken possession of the gas, it is immediately forwarded to the purchasing customer. Payment from the customer is then made into an Altra Escrow account, from which the disbursal to the seller is made, minus Altra's transaction fees. In this way, by serving as the intermediary in the transaction, Altra assumes any risk in the transaction and is able to guarantee that the seller will actually deliver, that the buyer will accept the delivery and that the buyer will pay for the delivered product.

The types of intermediated models similar to that of Altra Energy support an environment where there are many potential suppliers and many potential buyers. In these cases maximizing liquidity are goals 1, 2, and 3. Critical to achieving and maintaining liquidity is the perception by both sides of the transaction (i.e., the buyer and seller) of the exchange's neutrality. If either party were to feel the exchange was working against them, certainly they would be unlikely to trust their business to it. As a result, information transparency is critical, requiring both parties to view complete bidding activity in real-time. In this regard, the mechanics of a bidirectional exchange are particularly effective in remaining neutral and can, therefore, serve and support each of the parties in the transaction in an apparently fair manner. In other exchange models, however, the exchange is working on behalf of one of the parties in particular. These exchanges enable trading practices to follow specific auction models that move in a single direction.

Auctions—Engines of Liquidity

The behavior of exchanges is often driven by the auction engines that power them. The most common is the bidirectional bid/ask model discussed earlier, where the exchange acts the intermediary between multiple buyers and sellers, serving as the market maker or host of the transaction, and remaining neutral on price fluctuations (e.g., the market sets the price). Other models, however, focus on one specific orientation, either the buyer or seller.

Auction models have evolved over the centuries and vary greatly in their impact on the business models they are applied to. Some auctions are defined by specific rules, such as the infamous Dutch auction originating from the mad tulip trading of the sixteenth century. Most interpretations of this model allow bidders to compete for the first opportunity to purchase a particular set of goods. The highest bidder receives the first chance to buy, typically at whatever quantity desired, then the second-highest bidder can purchase what remains, and so on. In the Dutch tulip auction, which is still held today, a lot of tulip bulbs is initially offered at a high price that is progressively lowered until a bid is made and the item sold. Bidders race against the clock and must submit bids before time expires (Figures 3.2a, 3.2b, and 3.2c).

Figure 3.2 (a)   The trading floor of an early Dutch Tulip Auction in Holland, one of the oldest ongoing business-to-business auctions in the world. Courtesy the Aalsmeer Flower Auction.

Figure 3.2 (b)   While the basic rules of the Aalsmeer Flower Auction have changed very little since it first opened in 1912, it has evolved into a highly automated operation with spoilage (flowers not sold) reported as less than 0.5% per year. Reproduced with acknowledgment from Aalsmeer Flower Auction.

Figure 3.2 (c)   The Aalsmeer Flower Auction is recognized by the *Guinness Book of World Records* as both the world's largest auction house and the largest commercial building, covering 766,000 square meters or the equivalent of 125 football fields. Reproduced with acknowledgement from Aalsmeer Flower Auction.

In general, however, the behavior of auctions is determined by the orientation of sellers to users, whether many-to-many as in the case of the bidirectional exchange, or those that are initiated by just one buying party or selling party.

The business model of each exchange is typically defined by the orientation of buying parties to selling parties at the time the transaction is consummated (not during the bidding process, where there might be multiple parties involved that never ultimately participate in the transaction). For the purpose of illustration, we will discuss auctions in the context of four distinct categories (Figure 3.3):

1. The English or forward auction, involving multiple buyers with one seller;
2. The reverse auction, enabling instant monopsonies (literally a market with only one buyer), where multiple sellers compete for the business of a single buyer;
3. The cooperative auction, combining multiple buyers into a single transaction with a single seller;

	Single Buyer	Multiple Buyers
Multiple Sellers	• Reverse Auctions • RFP/RFQ (multivariate decisions) • Prices Only Go *Down* • FreeMarkets.com, OnVia, CreditTrade • Typically Sealed Bid • Faster Conversion Rates	• Bid/Ask Model • Typically Anonymous Transactions • *Bi-directional* Price Change (up and down) • Intermediary Arbitrage and Settlement • Altra Energy, NECX, NASDAQ • Fastest Conversion Rates
Single Seller	• Forward or English Auction • Typically Public Price Disclosure • Prices Only Go *Up* • Favors Perishables and Surplus • DoveBid, I-comindustry.com, AdAuction • Slow Conversion Rates	• Cooperative and Aggregated Buying • Prices *Down* as Buyers/Orders *Increase* • Mirrors Off-line Buyer Consortiums (GPOs) • High Leverage for Market-to-Market Deals • Mercata, MetalSite, Private Infomediaries • Slow Conversion Rates

Figure 3.3   The type of auction used and the behaviors that result are most often determined by the relationship of the number of buyers to the number of sellers as shown here.

4. The bid/ask model powering the bidirectional exchange, joining multiple buyers with multiple sellers.

Feeding Frenzy—The Traditional English Auction

The most commonly known auction model is the English auction where, as shown on the earlier matrix, a single market maker facilitates multiple bids on behalf of a single seller, resulting in a transaction with one buyer. Thus this is a one-to-one model where the market maker either sells a product on behalf of the seller (think Sotheby's) or an indirect seller such as a sell-side commerce portal uses the auction model to sell slowly moving products.

Given the traditional association of English auctions with surplus merchandise sold at what is comparably below market prices, there is a perception of the opportunity for a "deal" with these types of exchanges. The mechanics of this auction model, however, most greatly benefit the seller. This is due to the fact that by definition there are multiple buyers for each seller, prices only move up with the English auction.

The types of markets where these auctions add the greatest value is where there is a high degree of perishability with the products being sold. For example, AdAuction is a market maker for advertisements in print, radio, and television media. When a selling party brings ad space to market, it has effectively conceded that the commodity cannot be sold through the conventional market. Ads of course are valuable only for fixed periods of time, until the time slot has expired or the issue date has run.

As a result of this, ad sellers would likely see much greater returns per transaction sold through an anonymous bidirectional exchange. This would require a critical mass of buyers for the specific slots and demographics being offered. Given the near impossibility of this, AdAuction uses the English auction model by posting what ads are available and selling them to the highest bidder. Typically a minimum threshold is put in place representing the lowest acceptable price or minimum bid as the starting point. For AdAuction, this is the threshold whereby anything less will represent the ad being run as a bonus to a paying advertiser, but anything over this is incremental revenue, even if it adds only pennies on the dollar to the going market rate.

Another good example (highlighting the perishability condition) is GoFish. (GoFish is a seafood exchange and is discussed in greater detail in Chapter 4.)

In this way, exchanges using this model address inefficiencies within markets by "selling the unsalable." This also applies to nonperishable surplus goods. Exchanges such as DoveBid and I-comindustry.com act as liquidators by selling surplus industrial equipment on behalf of companies that have fully depreciated it and need to upgrade or, for other reasons, are not able to use the surplus. This type of business model has existed forever, and DoveBid, in particular, has been around for decades.

What had happened in the past, however, was that auctions were held on site at a specific physical location and the market was limited to whoever happened to show up. With an online exchange, the marketmaker is able to move beyond such geographic limitations and leverage the global market provided by the Internet. This has the effect of broadening the potential purchasing audience for the seller, whose buyers are no longer constrained by travel requirements and cost, and by limited hours-of-operation or differing time zones. For efficient online auctions, however, the exchange marketplace must find some means to create demand around a specific auction event.

One driver for demand is to limit the auction to a specific time interval, thereby introducing the concern that a product be sold before the prospective buyer has a chance to bid, but also that the ability to bid exists for only a limited time. As buyers participating in this model most often represent bargain hunters and often do not have any specific time sensitivity associated with the transaction, products sold through English auctions typically involve slower conversion rates (time from offering to settlement) and often require this type of prodding.

Cooperative Bidding—Defying Economic Gravity

Another approach, which is fairly new, defies economic gravity by lowering prices as demand increases. The best-known example of this model is Mercata, made famous by its marketing campaign featuring commercials where individuals stand around cheering as the price for the product they ordered drops as other buyers sign-up after them.

The exchanges act as demand aggregators, first acting as a buy-side marketmaker to collect orders, then finding the best price for the bundled purchase. The most common approach is to work with a fixed set of products available at tiered prices. Buyers can browse current prices on specific products and offer bids on specific products, then the market maker determines if the sum of all bids is within the range of the pre-negotiated price at that quantity.

To illustrate this model, imagine that 100 individuals make offers that average $550 on a particular laptop listed on the site, and the marketmaker negotiated a purchase of 100 laptops for $50,000. Since the aggregate bid for the 100 laptops is $55,000 and above the price prenegotiated by the exchange, everyone within that group who bid, "wins" at their individual bid price, and the marketmaker pockets the difference of $5,000.

This can be an effective model for indirect sales of off-the-shelf products, but difficult for made-to-order purchases, where each individual's requirements would be difficult to normalize into a single requirement. Given the complexity of this auction model, it also presents one of the slowest conversion rates.

A second approach that is better suited for RFQ-driven, made-to-order purchase processes is the single-buyer to many-seller model of the reverse auction model. Within this model, the exchange creates a monopsony (the single buyer equivalent of a monopoly) by facilitating competition among multiple sellers for the business of a single buyer. This model most closely resembles the traditional approach of large buyers, such as GE (discussed next), however, smaller organizations would otherwise find it nearly impossible to generate on their own the degree of leverage offered by the reverse auction model within the context of an online exchange. One of the most robust examples of the reverse auction model is FreeMarkets.

The Power of Monopsonies: Leveraging Reverse Markets

"Where does the Internet rank in priority? It is Number 1, and Number 2, Number 3, Number 4." In late 1994, five years before Jack Welch uttered these now famous words, a freshly minted MBA named Glen Meakem presented what must have seemed a farfetched new business model to General Electric's senior management at its headquarters in Fairfield, Connecticut. Meakem's career had been defined by purchasing, from his role as a procurement officer in the Army Reserve to the focus of his work as an associate at McKinsey to, ultimately, his role at GE—an unlikely destination for an aggressive young Harvard MBA, but nonetheless his first choice.

There, Meakem observed firsthand GE's old-world method of selecting suppliers through on-site auctions that are part cattle drive, part Turkish bazaar. With a mindset permanently tuned toward purchasing efficiency, Meakem envisioned a model of holding the supplier auctions electronically, creating a one-sided NASDAQ-like market for industrial supplies where each purchase would be put up to bid by a competing group of sellers—a process known as a *reverse auction.* In the pre-Web era of 1994, the idea was to hold auctions over the General Electric Information Services (GEIS) private supplier network. That year Meakem's idea was run with mixed results as a fully functional prototype; however, he did prove the concept and, in the process, was able to capture notable cost savings through cheaper supplier selection.

Results in hand, Meakem pitched the idea to an audience of top GE brass, which included CIO Gary Reiner, his supervisor at the time. Yet the group was unable to warm up to what was perceived as a risky venture, with an expected cost of approximately $10 million to set up. Two months later, with his idea shot down, Meakem left GE and a new venture named FreeMarkets was hatched. By the time Welch had the Internet epiphany that inspired his quote, FreeMarkets had gone public and was worth over $10 billion dollars, nearly 4 percent of GE's market cap—the world's most valuable company.

FreeMarkets represents one of the first exchange applications of the reverse auction model. This concept should be familiar to anyone who has used *Priceline.com,* the consumer purchasing system that allows individuals to specify their buying criteria and then have multiple suppliers bid for their business. This is distinct from the traditional notion of an auction, the forward or English auction, where multiple buyers bid on the single seller's offering. An obvious difference is that the latter favors the seller, as prices only rise or at worst remain static. With the reverse auction, prices decline in favor of the buyer, as is the case with FreeMarkets, or as with Priceline, allowing the buyer to set the price, and the first seller willing to match it is selected (or if a seller bids less, Priceline pockets the difference).

> GE's old-world method of selecting suppliers was through on-site auctions that were part cattle drive, part Turkish bazaar.

Perhaps less apparent is the greater control the reverse auction offers the buyer over parameters other than price. For example, a buyer looking to purchase off-the-shelf products like office supplies can search across various traditional auction sites to find an opportunity to bid the best deal, and in this case can take advantage of special circumstances such as a supplier's need to liquidate a particular lot of merchandise. Computer equipment reseller TechData uses auctions to quickly sell excess merchandise for pennies on the dollar, presenting great opportunities for buyers not bound by time constraints. Leveraging the efficiencies of online markets, TechData is able to sell products at a considerable discount, yet still command a higher price for the individual buyer than would be possible through the traditional means of offline liquidation.

For a manufacturer looking to secure suppliers for individually crafted components, the situation is quite different. Not only is timing an issue, but many other parameters come into play that are not typically part of an off-the-shelf purchase. For this reason, the traditional means of supplier selection is not through anonymous auctions but through an often-tedious process of developing and distributing requests for quotation (RFQs).

This process itself presents transactions costs, the direct costs of developing and reviewing RFQs and responses, as well as the inherent risk in selecting an unknown supplier. For this reason, manufacturers require sufficient economic incentive to switch suppliers and go through the bid process. For the supplier, the bidding process is almost always done in the dark (How would they know what their competitors are bidding?) and consequently most offer a best guess as to variable factors such as price and delivery. It is a widely recognized truism that sealed-bid scenarios almost always favor the seller, where there is no visible price competition. As a result of these factors, incumbent suppliers are typically overwhelmingly favored, and thereby feel little competitive pressure with existing clients.

Here is where the reverse auction model can offer real value to the buyer, by handing over control of the definition of bidding parameters and introducing greater competition by completely exposing the bidding process. This is accomplished by first standardizing every line item in the RFQ. This requires a standard response on every aspect including specific products and materials, but also the production and delivery schedule, payment terms, inventory arrangements, and all aspects specified by the RFQ.

By tightly controlling all parameters other than price, then displaying responses in a public forum, reverse markets are able to generate a great deal of competition to what is typically a complex and otherwise locked-up process.

An additional benefit of this approach is the ability to develop an economy of scale by bundling multiple buyers into one offer for sellers to bid on. Reverse markets facilitate this by providing a standard approach to bid solicitation, allowing each buyer's requirements to be entered once and assessed by multiple sellers. Reciprocally, this allows multiple buyers to benefit from an economy of scale where matching requirements are aggregated into one bid. The exchange manages the process of compiling the single bid, with the resulting seller typically managing the dissemination of the production lot among the buyers.

By adding these capabilities to collaborative communities and vertical aggregators, the value of the reverse market is further enhanced through services such as assistance with RFQ development, prequalification of potential bidders, and other allied services such as letters of credit, logistics support, and import/export facilitation. While exchange marketplaces such as FreeMarkets are just starting to touch on these areas, this will be a hot point of competitive differentiation in the future. Today, for example, FreeMarkets charges buyers a fixed subscription fee, while giving sellers a free ride. Others charge sellers, who simply build this fee into their bid. Both approaches, which essentially represent a transaction fee, will experience price competition from the growing number of exchanges that offer this capability. This will result in a substantial reduction or outright elimination of fees on both sides, and revenue will come solely from value-added services, and, in some cases, a percentage of cost savings by either party through greater operational efficiencies.

The Exchange Evolution

... the modern organization is a destabilizer ... it must be organized for the systematic abandonment of whatever is established, customary, familiar, and comfortable, whether that is a product, a service, or a process; a set of skills; human and social relationships; or the organizations itself. In short, it must be organized for constant change.

Peter Drucker

A misconception that surrounds the notion of the X-economy exchange is that it is defined as discrete, online transactions between anonymous participants; that within the exchange buyers will reap great gains in efficiency by clobbering their best suppliers until they acquiesce to great discounts on products sold previously at what is presumed to have been greatly inflated rates; that online auctions will pit product against product, where the real winner is the lucky buyer who enjoys a manyfold discount on the purchase of the supplies and materials necessary to run his business.

While there is a kernel of truth to these misconceptions about exchanges, the reality is that each of these notions is fundamentally flawed.

Enabled by a level operational efficiency and degree of access heretofore unachievable in the offline world, online auctions and their result of dynamic pricing will, and indeed have already begun to, revolutionize many areas of business. But this should not come at the expense of existing supplier relationships.

> It is a point of fact that no matter how much has changed in the "new economy," business is still a function of the same reciprocal, collaborative negotiation process that defined the ancient Souk of centuries ago and has held true for the multinational trade of today.

Consider your own business for a moment. Whether you are a manufacturer or another enabler along the chain of events which moves products from concept to production, it is highly unlikely you will benefit from a business environment devoid of continuity or persistence of relationship. This is what separates the X-economy exchange from consumer-to-consumer auction models such as eBay.

Although eBay has attempted forays into the world of business-to-business exchanges, it is highly unlikely you would look to this site as the source for the critical ingredients of your business. Consumer sites such as eBay are an appropriate replacement for weekend flea markets and garage sales, but without the ability to maintain a sense of trust and community among trading partners, it is wholly insufficient for business-to-business commerce. What is lacking is the community. With over 20 million users, eBay brags to be "bigger than New York City." Imagine New York as a city comprised entirely of shut-ins, without telephones or a central directory, and only the ability to connect through serendipitous encounters online. That may do wonders for crime prevention, but it is no way to build a community.

Business is not conducted within impersonal anonymous environments, but sitting on barstools, working on the back of napkins, and negotiating on the golf course. It is a point of fact that no matter how much has changed in the "new economy," business is still a function of the same reciprocal, collaborative negotiation process that defined the ancient Souk of centuries ago and has held true for the multinational trade of today.

While it is undeniable that the Internet has put into motion the redefinition of virtually every aspect of the way we work, the true potential of the X-economy exchange will only be realized once the online world is able to represent with full fidelity the traditional structure of relationships that has evolved in the offline world for the last 5,000 years.

> Imagine New York as a city comprised entirely of shut-ins, without telephones or a central directory, and only the ability to connect through serendipitous encounters on line. That may do wonders for crime prevention, but it is no way to build a community.

The evolution from brick-and-mortar with a Web site to a true X-economy exchange represents a continuum with six distinct, yet overlapping stages. Each one builds on the other, bringing together an increasing number of constituencies and capabilities, and at each stage offering an exponentially greater value proposition by reinforcing existing relationships and trading communities, not seeking to replace them with every executed transaction.

These six stages (Figure 3.4) are:

1. The electronic billboard
2. The virtual community
3. The commerce portal
4. The vertical aggregator
5. The infomediary
6. The vortal

The *electronic billboard* focuses on vertical industry segments looking for specialized content about products and companies specific to that community and has a revenue model built on the assumption that commercial transactions will continue to be executed offline, but product manufacturers will pay for the right to put their content in front of potential buyers visiting the exchange.

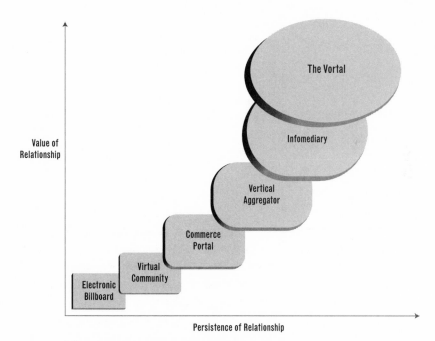

Figure 3.4   As the persistence of the relationship between partners and customers increases, so does the value of the relationship. This is often referred to as the "lifetime value" of a customer. Exchanges can create this persistence even when the individual partners of a value chain change often.

The *virtual community* offers a centralized point of collaboration for constituents within a particular area of interest, ranging from construction projects to the ownership of specialized products. The business model of this exchange is built around the notion that community members will pay for access to another, and value is created through both the facilitated exchange of information between constituents and availability of an online platform for collaboration.

The *commerce portal* offers a centralized resource for the online purchasing of multiple manufacturers' products through a single intermediary. The exchange builds value by integrating with the processes of trading constituents, reducing the barriers and transactional inefficiencies presented by the traditional purchasing process.

The *vertical aggregator* presents a vertical industry platform for the many otherwise disparate activities involved in commercial trade, ranging from following industry news to sourcing suppliers to enabling and fulfilling transactions.

The *infomediary*[1] redefines the concept of collaborative bidding by leveraging the commercial needs of a community by aggregating these into a set of bundled transactions. But rather than waiting for each individual constituent to speak out, the infomediary uses its knowledge of each community members needs and proactively assembles products and services uniquely tailored to them at the time of delivery, yet leverages the collective bargaining advantage from aggregating multiple transactions of this type to reap greater efficiency when sourcing suppliers.

The *vortal* builds on the industry focus of the vertical aggregator and the intimate knowledge of community found with the infomediary and creates a fluid environment supporting the rapid assembling of value chains. The vortal represents the furthest evolution of the exchange model, providing a true vertical platform for all commercial activity, from design to negotiation to production.

Across the continuum of X-economy exchanges, the value proposition for each model is defined in terms of the ability to cultivate and

---

[1] John Hagel III and Marc Singer, *Net Worth: Shaping Markets When Customers Make the Rules*, Boston, MA: Harvard Business School Press, 1999.

nurture a self-sustaining community, and the ability to translate this into economic benefit. This positions each stage of the exchange model according to two dimensions: *persistence of relationship* and *realization of value.*

The remainder of this chapter is dedicated to exploring each of these stages in greater detail, examining them in terms of, their strengths, weaknesses and roles in delivering or maintaining competitive edge. But one last caveat before we start.

Although the exchange marketplace has been subject to significant market volatility, resulting in no small part from the collapse of the dot-com phenomenon, the lessons to be learned from the pioneering players in this space are no less important. It is clear that failure, success, and consolidation will be difficult to predict with precision at such an early stage. Imagine trying to pick the winners in any incipient industry from the dozens of very smart and ambitious pioneers who shape a new market. Whether it be early twentieth-century car manufacturers or late twentieth-century exchanges, odds are that only hindsight will offer the 20/20 vision hidden somewhere in the cases and pages that follow.

The Electronic Billboard

In the mid-1990s, the advertising salesman of a trade magazine focused on the sewage treatment industry envisaged how radically his world would change in the near future. Working in the deepest annals of offline B2B commerce, this salesman, Mike McNulty, recognized the threat posed by the Web to his own livelihood. Shortly thereafter, he led the launch of what was to become the first publicly traded exchange. From this unlikely beginning, VerticalNet, Inc. was launched as one of the first examples of the Stage One exchange business model—the Electronic Billboard.

Prior to the Web, vertical trade publications such as McNulty's WaterWorld offered what was at the time a uniquely targeted channel for manufacturers to reach dedicated enthusiasts of such matters as sewage treatment and hydraulic pumps. By the mid-1990s, however, it was clear that these vertical trade publications were rapidly losing their proprietary hold on trading communities as the Web offered the chance for manufacturers to directly communicate with the market.

> For the electronic billboard, content is not "king," as goes the rallying cry of many other information-based business models.

Recognizing the emergence of the disintermediating effect of the Web was not unique to McNulty nor was it particularly visionary even in 1995, the year VerticalNet was founded. McNulty's vision, however, was to reintroduce the intermediary as the central coordinating entity for vertical trade information. An important distinction between the initial VerticalNet business model, which represents the definitive profile of the electronic billboard, and other information-based business models both then and now, is in terms of both how content is handled and from where revenue is derived. As is explained in greater detail next, VerticalNet has built a multimillion dollar business by redefining the notion of advertising. This involves reintermediating the publishing business model by redirecting to VerticalNet readers who might otherwise use traditional publications to find product information. VerticalNet instead serves as the central destination point for seller-produced and provided content. This distinction is at the heart of the electronic billboard business model.

The electronic billboard has none of the journalistic aspirations of other business models. Such is the case for Cahners' Manufacturing.net which has been positioned to compete directly with VerticalNet in the manufacturing space. Although Manufacturing.net was very closely tied with Cahners' offline vertical publications, it has sure made signficant inroads. Cahner's originally feared the cannibalization of other offline publishers businesses. There was also the issue of journalistic integrity. Initially, attempts such as Cahners' failed to achieve the commercial success that VerticalNet had with the electronic billboard model (see below for a detailed description of VerticalNet's performance). Lately, however, the tide has turned to favor, or at least level the playing field for, incumbents who build exchanges as spin-offs of established businesses. Still, understanding the evolution of exchanges requires starting with the electronic billboard.

For the electronic billboard, content is not "king," as goes the rallying cry of many other information-based business models. Rather content is viewed as the tenant of virtual real estate over which the exchange, such as VerticalNet, is the landlord. As a result, the revenue model of the electronic billboard is not cyclical, where an advertisement would be displayed for only a specific time interval, but instead a matter of renting space for an extended period. This allows a compounding of revenue growth, by creating an expanding group of content providers, rather than seeking to fill a discrete number of advertisement opportunities.

Traditionally, the role of market information provider was expected to be an impartial third party, clearly separating itself from proprietary content from advertisers. Trade publications, for example, the perennial source of market data in the old economy, went to great lengths to demonstrate their lack of bias to specific advertisers. In the X-economy, however, the speed of market change has led community participants to prioritize the ability to quickly find consistent and comprehensive information. Successful businesses following the electronic billboard model recognize this, creating a highly verticalized environment with a standard format and consistent look and feel across all content.

This orientation is very different from that of traditional publishing business models, where a clear separation between journalistic and advertising content must be maintained. The significance of this difference, however, should not be overlooked. The success of the electronic billboard is not simply a matter of the lack of separation between the two, but rather that both forms of information must be seamlessly integrated. The site must be more than aggregated information but must also be designed in such a way as to articulate the unique language of the industry sector around which it is branded.

The electronic billboard is not a publishing business model, however, nor is it the Yahoo! approach of building Web directories. By definition, this latter approach represents links to other Web pages, and as such, away from the marketplace. The ability to monetize these links is limited to charging for click-throughs or inclusion in the directory.

This limitation presents an inherent lack of continuity and a fundamental limitation of the business models value proposition—value is created only when users leave the site. By contrast, the electronic billboard model presents an inclusive destination site designed to scale to a vast virtual real estate empire.

> The electronic billboard's revenue model focuses on paid real estate for the display of free content.

Folklore has it that when the infamous 1930s criminal John Dillinger was asked why he robbed banks, he replied (logically), "Because that's where the money is." The electronic billboard model allows exchanges to follow the same strategy. Since the revenue model is based on paid inclusion of sponsors' content within the site, rather than by click-throughs or other user/buyer transactions, exchanges can scale quickly by aggressively selling sponsors. While the money ultimately lies with the buyer, it is the seller who pays for access to the buyer. And like banks, sellers are easier to find. The exchange will quickly zero in on the major players within a specific vertical, first signing-up the key (and often largest) players within the segment, creating demand among the remaining competitors who won't want to be left out of the action. Now with the majority of product and service providers locked-up, the exchange has a compelling destination site with which to attract potential buyers—where else can you find a comprehensive source of information on all the products and services that drive your own industry?

The result is a winner-takes-most model where the site that is first to lock-up a critical mass of industry players has a major advantage over any potential competitor. The result for any segment is a race that is run in (at least) one of two directions. First is signing up as many participants as possible. Second is to further define the segment by increasing levels of granularity. For example, from manufacturing in general to electronics manufacturing or specifically semiconductors. For VerticalNet, this has evolved from the original site conceived by McNulty, WaterOnline.com, to over 55 separate vertically oriented sites across 10 industry sectors hosting over 2,500 individual "storefronts," where manufacturers and services providers pay an annual rental fee ranging from $5,000 to $15,000.

VerticalNet's Vertical Exchanges and Storefronts

While VerticalNet recognized many of the differences between the traditional publishing industry model and that of the electronic billboard business model, there are several aspects of its market strategy that offer parallels. VerticalNet pursued a portfolio strategy of building and buying tightly focused exchanges that it has labeled *Vertical Trading Communities* built around such industries and specialized markets as oil and gas utilities, digital broadcasting, embedded technology, pharmaceuticals, and food services. After the initial WaterOnline site, selection of subsequent segments had little to do with internal domain expertise, but rather was based on a set of well-defined criteria concerning market behavior and composition:

1. Each target industry segment must consist of annual revenue of at least $8 billion with annual advertising spending of no less than $10 million.
2. The market structure must be fragmented without a single dominant buyer or seller, be global in nature, and consist of Web-savvy participants.
3. Sellers in the market must demonstrate competitive innovation through a history of new product and service introductions, and the majority of seller revenue should come from new purchases, rather than from maintenance or other aftermarket services.

Unlike the analogy of the tree that strengthens its position by driving its roots deep into the ground, the more appropriate metaphor for VerticalNet is the vine that finds an entry point through the forest canopy then spreads out horizontally, dropping its seedlings wherever it can find a fertile opening, and eventually strangling trees below it.

This criteria presents the optimal ecology for any online market-place, and particularly so for the electronic billboard. Since the electronic billboard model, by design, will compete with advertising dollars (just as the Web alone presents a competitive channel to traditional advertisements) it is vital that the market segment already offers a critical mass of addressable revenue. By targeting competitive verticals with many players and frequent turnover of products, VerticalNet can exploit the demand for communicating product data to a target audience thirsty for up-to-date industry information. And by focusing on Web-savvy vertical segments, VerticalNet can expand quickly without having to worry about industrywide infrastructure issues that would otherwise seriously impede growth.

Perhaps less obvious, however, but most critical to VerticalNet, is how this criteria relates to VerticalNet's portfolio strategy. If Vertical-Net were to focus only on the sewage treatment industry vis-à-vis WaterOnline, then these issues would be less important than the basic need to dominate the segment, driving it to further differentiate by offering deeper levels of industry-focused services. But VerticalNet's portfolio approach dictates a strategy that, at least initially, must be a "mile wide and an inch deep." Unlike the analogy of the tree that strengthens its position by driving its roots deep into the ground, the more appropriate metaphor for VerticalNet is the vine that finds an entry point through the forest canopy then spreads out horizontally, dropping its seedlings wherever it can find a fertile opening, and eventually strangling trees below it.

Detractors of VerticalNet have criticized the portfolio approach as too shallow and thereby vulnerable to competitive plays offering more sophisticated e-commerce capabilities.

This concern applies to any exchange using the electronic billboard model. But closer examination reveals other challenges as well. VerticalNet's initial growth was a function of perfecting the electronic billboard model within the initial vertical exchanges, such as WaterOnline, then finding subsequent segments meeting the criteria above where they can be quickly replicated. This was further driven by leveraging an aggressive sales force with experience selling to small- to medium-sized manufacturers accustomed to buying advertising space in vertically oriented publications.

VerticalNet built its early momentum during the first few years of its existence by remaining at a relatively superficial level providing sponsored content and not becoming involved directly in the selling process. As a result, it did not encounter the resistance from sellers' existing channels encountered by other exchanges, whose growth have been limited by the fear of alienating the sellers' largest revenue source. This has allowed VerticalNet to sign-up more participants than virtually any other exchange. This also presents a challenging paradox for VerticalNet's long-term growth strategy.

> The challenge to the electronic billboard model is the growth of the community of sponsors without eroding its vertical focus.

To expand revenue while remaining within the electronic billboard model, VerticalNet must either continue to grow the number of segments it addresses or increase the rate it charges for storefront participation. The latter is not a viable approach, as competitive forces are already putting downward pressure on the fees it's able to charge for sponsorship. Growing the number of markets it addresses will likely remain part of VerticalNet's strategy; however, the number of segments that meet the criteria listed above limits the degree to which it can rely on this strategy. Going outside of this group will inevitably result in higher operating costs and slower revenue growth, both being particularly undesirable in the face of declining sponsorship fees.

In light of this, VerticalNet faces the same limitation fundamental to the electronic billboard model, which necessitates other sources of revenue to maintain a growth trajectory, and in most cases, to reach profitability. The most likely source is to participate in sales transactions facilitated by the site. For VerticalNet, internal research has determined that approximately 20 percent of prospective buyers visiting their collective sites made a purchase within 6 months of visiting, averaging $25,000 per transaction. By charging a transaction fee of 1 percent to the seller, each of the roughly 2,500 participants would have to average 24 annual sales to equal the revenue VerticalNet now charges for storefront participation. This is not an unreasonable expectation, however, it introduces a number of new challenges to the electronic billboard model.

Selling VerticalNet's exchanges as commerce sites introduces greater complexity than the current sales force is accustomed to, having now to contend with overcoming the fear of disintermediation as well as selling a solution requiring integration with back-end systems. As will be discussed later, VerticalNet has already begun taking steps in this direction. To succeed in this highly competitive climate, however, it is necessary to establish relationships with partners more capable of selling and deploying these more complex solutions and services.

A pressing issue for any electronic billboard, however, is the need to strengthen its ties with the community of potential buyers. The fear is that commerce will take place offline, or otherwise outside of the exchange environment, and as a result little attention is paid to building the type of trust required to coax online commerce. For consumer commerce, this is often a matter of simply overcoming resistance to providing confidential payment information over the Internet. For the B2B world, however, the matter is much more complex. Consider the last major purchase you made on behalf of your company. Was your decision based solely or even primarily on price and availability? If so, it is unlikely the consequences of such a purchase played a large role in your career options. In those cases where such a decision does make a difference, whether choosing a subcontractor for a single project or selecting a supplier for an extended period of time, many more factors weigh in than are presented in a simple consumer purchase.

> Consider the last major purchase you made on behalf of your company. Was your decision based solely or even primarily on price and availability? If so, it is unlikely the consequences of such a purchase played a large role in your career options.

Here underlies our fundamental precept of exchanges and specifically of the X-economy—it is more about community than simply the competitive forces that define a market in its purest, simplest sense. These communities are bound by trust and by history. It is rare that a supplier will be replaced simply to save pennies on the dollar. Yet the ability to leverage the ubiquity of Web-based technology to offer unprecedented high levels of interactivity and intimacy among partners provides new inroads for upstarts that threaten the otherwise entrenched incumbents along the value chain.

The value of community and the ability to leverage it for strengthening the bonds between value chain constituents presents an opportunity for both buyers and sellers to increase their competitive stature, leading to our next exchange business model—the *virtual community*.

The Virtual Community

The virtual community first evolved as a more interactive approach to leveraging collaborative capabilities of exchanges such as threaded discussion groups and personalized content—the "My" approach to content management is discussed later in the book. The primary objective of these sites is to create loyalty among users by offering personalized information, as well as providing an online meeting place to interact with others of like interests. Here value is created through the development of individual profiles, where the interests of potential buyers are mapped to related goods and services offered by the host site, or in some cases by affiliated third parties. For example, an equipment reseller might offer to create such a community for commercial clients to provide network services such as online help, recall/update notices, and so on. Using the personalization capabilities of the exchange, users of a particular line of product are "up-sold" or "cross-sold" through targeted ads in a way that is roughly analogous to the way Amazon.com or LandsEnd.com profile consumer buyers in order to provide them with personalized Web sites that suggest items the consumer is interested in based on buying habits.

> The business-to-consumer business model of paid banner ads faces the potential of lock-out to the business-to-business arena as organizations increasingly restrict employee access to site with ads.

One of the limitations of this model, however, is that the target audience of these communities, principally corporate users, are often sitting behind firewalls which block access to websites with banner ads. This is a trend that is on the uptake, not in decline. In response to fears that range from lost productivity to the public display of obscene content, organizations are increasingly putting restrictions on the type of material available through corporate Internet access. In many cases this includes blanket restrictions on sites with banner ads.

This restriction may have little impact on the consumer businesses whose revenue is predominantly based on click-through activity outside of core business hours. But for the business betting on a future of ad revenue from a business-specific audience, this trend is a potential killer. As such we are on the cusp of a sea of change away from ad revenue and toward other forms of capitalization of the community.

One migration path moves to the left of traditional banner ads by offering a personalized storefront based on individual preferences and other criteria contained within user profiles. A limitation of this model, however, is that the unique roles of the content provider and the product marketer are most often in conflict. Accordingly, any action that gives even the appearance of compromising this (such as the overt promotion of a specific product) would gravely undermine the value of this relationship, and as such any realizable value of the profile information by the host site. Consequently, this version of the virtual community business model is similarly constrained as the electronic billboard, where content is used to attract a group of buyers in the hope of capitalizing on some form of downstream, indirect revenue.

The second approach is to leverage the strength of a virtual community as both a content provider and commerce-enabled exchange. This model turns the notion of the electronic billboard on its head, which assumes community is built in anticipation of a purchase and sees little value in the aftermarket. In contrast, this new model serves first as an information resource for all aspects of a focused business need or industry vertical. These businesses leverage the power of positive feedback loops to build a self-perpetuating community of participants—which in turn represent a lucrative base of buyers.

An example of this model is TestMart. TestMart was launched in 1998 to address the opportunity of equipment sales and leasing for the test and measurement industry. Similar to VerticalNet and the other business models described earlier, TestMart uses vertical content to drive traffic to the site. Where it departs from these, and the other models discussed later in this chapter, is that it is neither purely an information resource, and thereby not held to the limitations above, nor is it foremost a product seller, which would inevitably taint the impartiality of the information provided. Within this new model, and in the case of TestMart, content is neither sponsored nor specifically written in anticipation of a purchase, but rather is the essential nutrient of a virtual community—the "plankton" if you will, of an information-based ecosystem.

TestMart is designed as a comprehensive reference site featuring an extensive databases of unique, information on over 9,000 test and measurement products from a variety of third party sources, normalized into a common format and repository. It includes contact and historical information on more than 500 manufacturers, as well as a reference library of information of particular interest to the community, such as calibration intervals, life cycles, and industry specific matters.

In the first stage of its evolution, this information was held close to the vest by TestMart, used only internally for TestMart personnel to judge the value of the equipment it sells and leases—which is the direct mechanism by which it makes money. TestMart held what it considered to be one of the most comprehensive sources of information in existence on test and measurement. This was viewed as a significant component of its intellectual property and a major source of its competitive advantage. Yet TestMart's use of this database, primarily for determining the value of the equipment it trades in, offered very little leverage of the information.

The market for test and measurement equipment lives and dies by product information. To purchase, use, and maintain equipment, engineers are forever scouring sources for not just manufacturer-published, but more importantly peer-validated data on matters such as device calibrations, production variances, and other information which may be meaningless to you and me but is the stuff that literally keeps engineers up at night.

The ability for communities to trade in this information is one of the fundamental drivers of the Internet. What is lacking with the use of e-mail and USENET discussion groups for collecting this information, however, is a single destination point for finding information. This opens the door for an intermediary to act as clearinghouse for industry data, and as such the hub of the community which consumes this information.

In 1999, TestMart underwent a significant change in strategy, which involved making public its once tightly held database of product information and industry data. The impact of this was far more significant than might have been immediately apparent. This information was the sort for which engineers spend their days and nights searching. Some estimate they average as much as 30 percent of their time looking for product information and data points which should by all rights be provided by manufacturers and suppliers, but far more often is something that engineers must ferret out on their own.

Had the information been merely press releases, product specs (from manufacturers' marketing efforts), editorial reviews, and some form of discussion groups, TestMart would have simply copied dozens of other sites, even within their own industry, and likely had little success at building a community. The core difference is in the type and manner of the information TestMart made available. The database of product information is exactly the sort that brings engineers together—the techie equivalent of recapping the big game Monday morning around the water cooler.

Engineers by trade must be able to quickly track down obscure bits of information needed to complete design, integrate components, or often simply to get the products they've bought to work as intended. By providing a source of the specific information these community members require to complete their work, TestMart offers not only a level to attract engineers but has indirectly enlisted their help in promoting the site. When asked by a colleague about a particular set of data, any engineer familiar with TestMart is likely to refer him directly to the site. In this way, TestMart has substantially increased the leverage on the information in its database, moving from using it only to squeeze a marginal increase in value from an existing customer, to fueling a viral marketing program that reaches many times more potential community members than would be possible through direct methods. Perhaps just as valuable, this viral aspect allows TestMart to connect with the type of individuals hardest to reach through traditional marketing channels: those engineers who would otherwise only go through a trusted colleague to find information.

> Prosumers are a critical ingredient to successfully commercializing the virtual community by taking the plankton of raw information and moving it up the food chain by validating it, adding to it, and in some cases creating it.

The shift from traditional commerce to community is an important dimension played by community members. When valued information and the activities of peer review replace commercial transactions as the central rallying point of an exchange, then community members move beyond status as simply buyers and sellers to *prosumers* as Alvin Toffler termed them—individuals who consume a product and through this process actually add value. Prosumers are a critical ingredient to successfully commercializing the virtual community by taking the plankton of raw information and moving it up the food chain by validating it, adding to it, and in some cases creating it. These community members add value to not only the information available, but validate the site by ensuring its content is that of greatest relevance to the community. This illustrates how an exchange is to derive gain from the highest possible leverage on the community through contributions by unaffiliated Subject Matter Experts (SMEs).

SMEs represent a type of *uber-prosumer* who are found in every community. When properly channeled, these individuals act as both honesty brokers, validating the integrity of the information promoted throughout the community, as well as an indirect resource for community members. By facilitating access to the insights of these individuals, community organizers are able to extend the collective value of the community as a resource, without incurring any additional direct cost.

While the risks of this approach should not be dismissed, it is easy to exaggerate the potential dangers of allowing an organization's value proposition to be defined by the knowledge and behavior of individuals outside its direct influence. These dangers, principally the lack of control, are most often outweighed by the benefits of creating a self-sustaining, organically growing community. This may at first seem a bit intimidating, but this is also the essence of all markets and communities. In every case organizations are at the mercy of individuals outside of their direct control. The difference here is channeling these individuals to provide the highest possible leverage of the community.

The End of the Free Lunch

Following the paid-sponsorship approach of VerticalNet and transaction fees charged by many other exchanges, the third revenue model is rooted in what might be an anachronism to the "information wants to be free" crowd. Despite the endurance of the Internet myth, nothing in this world is free; everything is a function of economic trade-offs. Organizations willing to allow personnel access to banner ads and other potentially nonproductive content have chosen to risk productivity loss in favor of "free" information. Others, however, are happier to charge for access than to risk such a loss. For these organizations, a virtual community entrance fee is preferable to exposing personnel to banner ads and other distracting content. Similarly for many exchanges, the trade-off of diluted brand recognition within the community presented by other companies' ads and other mechanisms which encourage visitors to leave the site is not worth the short gain of sponsorship revenue.

The downside risks of an advertising-based revenue model and the encouragement of e-commerce transactions, however, are not the only drivers of this new type of exchange. Many exchanges are starting to recognize that the collective value of the information across the community often exceeds the revenue that can be squeezed out of sponsorship business models or even from the execution of transactions alone. The new value proposition is one of access to proprietary content generated by both the community itself and from other third-party sources. This has led to the evolution of a new business model built on the notion of becoming a collaboration hub for virtual communities of interest and practice.

Two notable examples of this type of business model are Bidcom and Bricsnet. Both focus on the construction industry, targeting the improvement of operational efficiencies through consolidated project data and online project management services. Both provide software-based services, primarily deployed over the Web, to address various aspects of collaboration within commercial building, from the bidding process to facilities management. In regards to e-commerce transactions, both offered this capability well into the deployment of the e-marketplace site, but both also have positioned this foremost as a service to the community, and much less so a driver for building it.

Like TestMart, both sites offer an extensive database of vertically oriented product and industry information, enough to enable any user to deal directly with manufacturers and make purchases outside of the site. It is not likely that many community members will do this, not only out of loyalty to the community organizer, but as a result of the tools each has built in place to facilitate the process of buying and selling online. But if members did go elsewhere for purchases, it would have little impact on these businesses' bottom line. They are foremost about community, not commerce, and transaction fees from online sales make up only a small percentage of their revenue.

Even as transaction volume increases, this percentage is likely to remain as small or even decline (as a result of shrinking percentages exchanges are able to charge for online sales, which will be discussed later). The bulk of the revenue model is based on the price of admission to the community, and as a result, the value to these businesses is in growing the community, not necessarily in transaction volume. In both cases, this is not simply a matter of encouraging casual visitors to the site but emerging as the de facto collaboration hub for subgroups within the industry.

The Commerce Portal

The third exchanges model focuses specifically on the purchasing process. These exchanges, called *commerce portals,* focus on operational efficiency and measure success by transactional volume. Acting as the hub of the purchasing process, they focus on automating basic functions such as order processing, funds transfer, fulfillment, and logistics.

Once basic commerce capabilities are in place, the next stage is to rollout pre- and postsales business processes. These additional services offer further revenue opportunities, such as those associated with the outsourcing of procurement and fulfillment processes. This is critical to the commerce portal's competitive distinction, which is based largely on the simple premise of offering a more efficient way to conduct existing business practices. In most cases, the commerce portal is not introducing any radical new business processes, but rather offers an easier and more cost-effective way of buying and selling products in which organizations already trade.

This necessitates an environment capable of delivering both front-end capabilities, such as account maintenance and status monitoring, as well as integrating with back-end systems of suppliers for executing orders and managing inventory. These capabilities are leveraged to build loyalty among customers by being easy to do business with. For example, many commerce portals attempt to reduce procurement inefficiencies faced by buyers through the offering of account maintenance services and workflow automation for backend processes. While traditional e-commerce sites face the challenge of competition that is "only a click away," commerce portals use these capabilities to "lock-in" the buyer maximizing the effort involved in switching to another distributor.

Where the emphasis is placed, in terms of who pays what service and where the greatest incentive is offered, is defined by the orientation of the commerce portal. Specifically, whether it is organized in favor of buyers or sellers. In others, it is determined by which side of the equation is the most fragmented and would benefit most from consolidation through an exchange.

Industries with a greater number of buyers than sellers have been the first to deploy commerce portals. By definition, these are horizontal in focus, such as office supplies or maintenance repair and operation (MRO) supplies. Examples include Grainger.com and MRO.com, distributors of industrial and maintenance products. These sites are the electronic equivalent of brick-and-mortar retailers and resellers, profiting from a combination of the mark-up on products and a transaction fee charged to the suppliers participating in the sites.

While these sites participate in the information ecology, buyers are typically attracted by the availability of products, not the impartiality of the information presented. It is expected that any information provided serves the interest of the seller, and is most often oriented to reinforcing the purchase decision surrounding products available within the portal. Most businesses engaged in this type of exchange are existing commercial distributors of some sort, who have ported their business models to an exchange.

For industries dominated by a smaller number of buyers serviced by a large number of sellers, such as government or automobile manufacturing where about 20 buyers deal with over 100,000 suppliers, commerce portals are organized with a buy-side orientation, rather than the sell-side focus described earlier. These buyer-based communities have the inherent advantage of a built in market and typically focus on issues of supply chain management.

Leveraging Buyer-Based Communities

Although at age of 47 he was the youngest CEO in the history of General Motors, just a year prior to taking the helm in June 2000 of the world's largest company, Rick Wagoner rarely, if ever, used e-mail, nor did he even use a personal computer (by design his office wasn't equipped with one and his secretary was required to print his e-mail messages for his review). This Luddite type of existence was not unique to Wagoner or even GM management and was common among its partners and suppliers, the majority of whom did not utilize e-mail or the Internet in any form. In 1999, while consumer-oriented kiosks were letting individuals design their own cars, the auto industry as a whole was far from Internet savvy.

Arguably both the first and last network-based innovation in the auto industry began in the 1960s and reached its zenith in the 1980s. This innovation was the widespread deployment of electronic data interchange (EDI)—the proprietary standard for exchanging financial documents and inventory information. Compared to the dynamic and scalable Web-based technology and protocols such as XML, EDI is without question a dinosaur.

XML: X-Economy Holy Grail

Standards in practice and technology are a critical component of economic infrastructure. But they are also one of the most contentious arenas of any massive undertaking. Take for example the Chunnel, the underground tunnel that links Folkestone, England, with Coquelles, France.

When the notion of a Chunnel was revisited in 1986, what was originally envisioned was a multiuse facility that would accommodate both rail and motor traffic. An obvious problem with the latter is that it would then be possible to drive from England, where you would be on the left-hand side of the road, directly to France where they drive on the right. It is not difficult to imagine the contention that arose between the French and English committees arguing that the opposite country should adopt the driving practices of their own, giving new meaning to the notion of dealing with issues "head-on."

The initial compromise was to agree on a "phased-in" approach to standardization. Starting with trucks perhaps, then moving down to autos and motorcycles? Here is an illustration of both the needs for universal standards and the very real dangers of committee-led decision making. Thankfully, the final compromise was to place vehicles onto a train, where they can enter from the left side and exit from the right side.

The role these trains play in arbitrating well-entrenched standards of practice is directly analogous to relationship between EDI and XML. EDI is a longstanding incumbent in business-to-business transactions, as entrenched as any railroad tracks. Yet virtually every new online exchange initiative is rooted in XML.

XML (extensible markup language) is effectively an open standard of the World Wide Web Consortium (W3C) and the Internet Engineering Task Force (IETF). However, specific "flavors" are promoted by smaller, more focused groups, including those with competing interest (such as cbML and cXML, respectively promoted by Commerce One and Ariba). Of several XML variants, one of the most promising is ebXML a set of specifications that together enable a joint initiative of the United Nations's UN/CEFACT (the most commonly support EDI standard) and OASIS. XML is also being extended to other standards such as the UDDI (Universal Description, Discovery and Integration) Project, focused on standardizing conventions for maintaining product information and catalog structures, and backed by players such as Ariba and IBM.

With the emergence of XML, most observers have been quick to sing the swan song of EDI. But to write it off so quickly would be a mistake. To paraphrase Mark Twain, the death of EDI has been greatly exaggerated. One of the greatest misconceptions about EDI and Internet protocols such as XML is that they are locked in a two-way race, when indeed they are not mutually exclusive at all. For many industries, a successful X-economy strategy will require the pairing of EDI and XML. EDI is a well-entrenched incumbent and XML has a long way to go before it can lay claim to the same breadth of reach.

So where does this leave XML? Because EDI is so expensive to implement and so rigid to integrate with existing applications, XML may be the key to EDI's future. In order to scale to the level that e-business volume is expected to reach within the next few years, thousands of organizations otherwise excluded from EDI-based trading communities will need inexpensive access. Here XML will serve as a gateway, not a replacement, for EDI transactions.

The key is that XML and EDI must exist in a cooperative strategy that marries the two to extend the broadest possible reach of the trading community. This notion has created an interesting dilemma for companies such as GE eXchange Services (formerly GEIS) who today control the lion's share of the EDI hosting market. GE seems to have acknowledge that the widespread transition to XML within the coming years may be inevitable, demonstrated by a major marketing campaign promoting XML and a number of very large investments in XML-related technologies and companies. Yet, today, EDI still represents a multimillion dollar business for GE.

It should perhaps come as no surprise that a three-letter acronym whose mere presence on a business plan could be worth millions of dollars would fail to meet such inflated expectations. Nor that an incumbent technology would fall out of favor with pundits on whose innovation meters it registers somewhere between punch cards and the Minitel.

For GM and its vast network of suppliers and dealers, decades of investment in EDI have meant rigid standardization and integration of systems and processes. This has resulted in an exorbitantly high cost of entry into the network, ranging from $10,000 to $100,000 just to get started. But it also has allowed GM suppliers to use the same infrastructure to deal with other auto manufacturers. Delphi Automotive Systems, for example, is the largest supplier in the automotive industry and one of the biggest players in the supply chains of not just the Big Three (GM, Ford, DamlierChrysler), but of twenty+ other auto manufacturer customers.

Switching from EDI to a proprietary Web-based system would mean retooling financial and inventory operations for not only GM, but for all manufacturers who did the same. Such a move by GM might be disastrous for Delphi Automotive and its 30,000 other suppliers, but that is exactly what it did attempt to do in 1997. And predictably, the rest of the Big Three automakers, Chrysler and Ford, quickly followed suit. If the objective is to enable and nurture existing relationships, however, buyers are better served by focusing on ease of doing business than simply encouraging competition among suppliers.

GM's first major attempt to leverage the Internet for reining in suppliers was to utilize the outsourced procurement services of FreeMarkets (see *The Power of Reverse Markets* later in this chapter). For a community of suppliers who in 1997 had in most cases no more experience with the Internet than GM's Wagoner, this move was met with less than overwhelming enthusiasm. This not only introduced a new technology metaphor, FreeMarket's proprietary BidWare and BidServ software, but also introduced an even greater adversarial dimension to the supplier/manufacturer relationship by forcing suppliers to bid for each piece of business.

For new suppliers without a prior history with GM, this may have offered an attractive alternative to the high cost of entry to the EDI network. But for the existing supplier community, this was all stick and no carrot. The vast majority of business for GM is through suppliers with whom they have long-term relationships, and in many cases having made significant investments in (Delphi, for example, was once owned by GM). Reverse auction systems such as that offered by FreeMarkets do have their place in business and can contribute greatly to reduced fragmentation and increased efficiency across the supply chain. The GM experience should not be perceived as an indictment of the model as a whole. If the objective is to enable and nurture existing relationships, however, buyers are better served by focusing on the ease of doing business rather than simply encouraging competition among suppliers.

In this initiative, GM broke a fundamental rule of the X-economy—putting their own commercial interests in conflict with the community. Not surprisingly, it found little success and was abandoned in 1999. The relationship with FreeMarkets was dropped in favor of building its own commerce portal, called GM TradeXchange in partnership with Commerce One, with whom it had taken an equity interest earlier that year.

By connecting GM with its 30,000 suppliers, the TradeXchange was designed to manage GM's supply chain from end-to-end, to enable collaborative production planning and comanaged inventories, as well as to allow both GM and its suppliers to order everything from paperclips to brake pads.

In contrast to GM's FreeMarkets initiative, TradeXchange was designed with an eye toward operational efficiency, rather than on inter-supplier competition. It was also built on top of technology that integrated with existing EDI infrastructure (albeit with a bit of effort for each supplier, at their expense).

Predictably, within weeks of GM's announcement of TradeXchange, Ford announced a partnership with Oracle to create AutoXchange, its commerce portal to coordinate an estimated $80 billion (1999) in annual purchases from *its* 30,000 suppliers. Given the considerable overlap between the two groups of suppliers, they soon faced the grim prospect of having to support not only two separate proprietary systems, but as many other systems as there would be other manufacturers.

Initially, each had tried to out-partner the other. Ford's partnership with Oracle and, added later, Cisco Systems was as impressive as GM's partnership with Commerce One, but not to be outdone, each had added platform player after platform player to the mix, from IBM to SAP.

Ultimately, however, the infrastructure partnerships are less important than the level of supplier/manufacturer participation in determining the success of any commerce portal initiative. This time around, suppliers called in their cards and forced the emulsification the two portals, in the process rallying DaimlerChrysler, Renault, Nissan, Toyota, and all their respective affiliates that combined comprise the vast majority of the auto industry. The result of these automobile manufacturers, along with GM and Ford, was Covisint.

Competitive Keiretsu

The emergence of Covisint represents a new trend of competitive *keiretsu* or coalitions of both competitors and partners forming across many different industries, particularly those that are buyer heavy.

In the case of Covisint, the fact that two competing sites already exist adds to the challenge of integration, however, this effort will certainly be less than what would be required to integrate 30,000 to 60,000 suppliers with the disparate systems of more than twenty manufacturers.

The first major hurdle for Covisint before becoming operational was clearance by the Federal Trade Commission, who has viewed the collusion of competitors organizing to derive a lower price from suppliers as a potential anti-trust violation. In mid-1999, the FTC began to take notice of exchange activity and the potential collusion and price fixing by non-neutral sites owned and operated by multiple competitors. Unfortunately for Covisint, its high prominence and visibility placed it at the center of the FTC's radar screen (Figure 3.5). In September of 2000, initial clearance was granted for Covisint to proceed. However, this by no means guarantees that the pressure of regulatory compliance has been entirely relieved. All exchanges, and Covisint no less, remain under the watchful eye of potentially overzealous regulators who may be less sensitive to the new practices of the X-economy and at any time may interfere with the evolution of trade.

Then there is the name. Where TradeXchange and AutoXchange were so uninspired that neither company was able to copyright the names or secure them as URLs, the choice of Covisint is not just unusual but certainly enigmatic, if not all together awkward. According to the organization it is not entirely random but rather derived from ". . . the concepts of *CO*nnectivity, collaboration, communication, and co-operation to the *VIS*ibility and *VIS*ion that the *INT*ernet and the *INT*egration our solutions will provide, as well as the integrity with which we will conduct business and our international reach and resources, Covisint is a succinct expression of our promise to our customers." Now try to pronounce it (cō-vis-int).

Whatever the origins of the names for these commerce portals, the apparent ambivalence to marketing fundamentals is illustrative of the lack of competitive forces these sites face. Whatever political jockeying is involved in lining up partners, the one thing these exchanges are not worried about is wooing buyers. In each industry, dominated by only a handful of buyers, there is likely not enough room for more than one centralized purchasing entity. The size of the auto industry made it a likely first mover and a worthy test case for how other industries will likely respond. One of the first to follow suit has been the oil industry, which has already gone through many of the evolutions and political gyrations that produced Covisint.

Following their peers in the automotive industry, twenty of the top players in the oil industry have announced various exchange

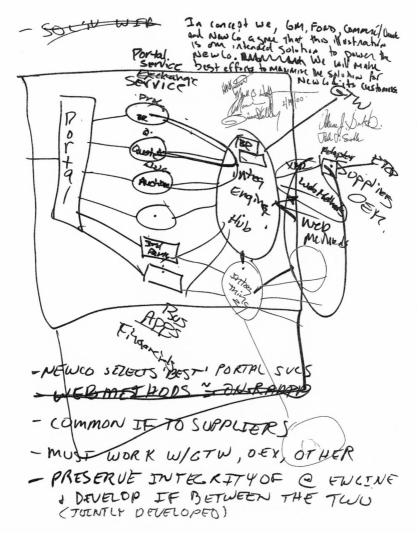

Figure 3.5 Initial handwritten sketch of the Covisint exchange from the first meetings with GM, Ford, Diamond Technology Partners, Oracle, and Commerce One. Some interesting notes on this include the reference to the Portal at the left of the diagram and the reference to the Hub (the center circle) which would constitute the engine of the exchange. Courtesy of Diamond Technology Partners.

initiatives focused specifically on supply process efficiencies. A difference in this case, however, is that the various exchange organizers have gone to lengths to pitch the value of the exchange framework for suppliers, emphasizing that the new form of interchange cannot be a zero sum game.

Part of this supplier-friendliness is a result of the lack of a single dominant controller of the global petrol supply chain (whereas Ford and GM combined arguably already had it locked for the auto industry). A top contender remains the most recently formed 14-company consortium, TradeRanger, representing the broadest reach so far across the petrol market's value chain, creating a framework for a significant commerce portal operation. The breadth of this particular initiative represents a significant opportunity for Commerce One, the exchange technology supplier, which will be able to benefit both from the initial exchange construction and its eventual IPO. Just as in the auto industry, the stakes are in the $100 billions for the portal that will handle all aspects of procurement related to the exploration, production, and distribution of oil and energy—from office supplies to oil rigs.

This activity can be seen across all industries, beginning with the largest and eventually trickling down to the most granular niche. The end result of these buy-side commerce portals is simply a standardized platform for purchases and will not eliminate the need for other aspects of trade and distribution channels. Once these sites reach dial-tone levels of ubiquity, where they can all plug and play neatly, this infrastructure will no longer offer any unique competitive advantage. Evolving in parallel in anticipation of this will continue to be other initiatives focused on matters such as collaborative design and demand-chain management. These aspects are discussed in further detail in the section on *vortals*.

Managing e-Catalogs—The Challenge of Sell-Side Commerce Portals

The catalog—not the lack of transaction processing software, not the lack of bandwidth to the home, not the lack of robust security, and not the lack of an appealing shopping experience—is what I believe is blocking the growth of Internet commerce today. Until businesses can easily produce and manage online catalogs, I don't think we'll see any of the dramatic growth forecasted by the compound annual growth algorithms embedded in industry pundits' spreadsheets.

Geoffrey Moore, author of *Crossing the Chasm*

Just as buy-side commerce portals work with a discrete number of buyers, sell-side commerce portals function as aggregators of a predetermined set of suppliers' product information. If prosaic on the surface, this issue represents one of the greatest technical challenges, as well as one of the largest areas of expense, involved with launching and maintaining an exchange. Here is why.

Unlike buy-side commerce portals, sell-side portals do not have a built-in community of buyers and as a result have to differentiate themselves across multiple dimensions, most notably: price, availability, and the ability to offer a better purchasing experience than the next alternative. Each one of these objectives is extremely information intensive.

The objective of any exchange is to minimize the degree of price-based differentiation which offers the weakest point of leverage for the seller. In the case of catalog aggregation, price is typically a matter beyond the control of the commerce portal as it is set by the supplier. Managing operating margin, however, is as much a function of catalog integration costs as it is market prices. The former is where the commerce portal has the greatest ability to control margin. Next to the wholesale costs of products themselves, the direct expense of integrating and maintaining e-catalogs is often the largest component of cost of goods sold. Of the $5 to $20 million reported for the initial deployment costs of commerce portals, typically more than half (often as much as 2/3) is associated with catalog integration costs. And unfortunately for the exchange owner, unlike software and design, these are almost entirely recurring costs.

The challenge for the sell-side commerce portal is that the cost of managing e-catalogs grows with other dimensions of differentiation as well. For example, ensuring product availability is a matter of having the right supplier relationships, back-end integration with supplier inventory systems, and multiple sources for a specific product. This often means managing individual relationships with literally thousands and in some cases even millions of SKUs (Stock-Keeping Unit—the classification scheme for individual products).

Clearly, the objective of any exchange is to minimize the degree of price-based differentiation, which offers the weakest point of leverage for the seller. The degree of complexity here is enormous. Imagine that you have manually integrated and validated entries for 500,000 different products from 1,000 different suppliers. What is the likelihood that something has changed in the time it took you to get from product 1 to product 500,000? This is the problem with catalogs: Things change. Products are updated or discontinued, prices fluctuate, design flaws are found and products are recalled. If only 15 percent of the catalog information must be updated each quarter, which would be an extraordinarily low amount, than more than half of the initial validation effort must be repeated each year.

The real value-add of the e-catalog is not the availability of information alone, but rather confidence in the ability to execute a comprehensive query from a single source.

The business model of the commerce portal carries with it an Internet-era expectation set among buyers. Specifically, customers expect real-time answers and inventory availability. Whereas when dealing with a paper catalog there is an expected degree of information latency, in the online world an e-catalog with out-of-date or otherwise inaccurate information is an abomination. It is therefore quite unfortunate that most suppliers have an offline orientation where updates are made only at specific intervals, and critical product alerts are issued as "pink sheets" sent out to catalog holders, often only after the distributor has promoted erroneous information among prospects and customers.

As a result, the most common form of catalog integration today is to take the proprietary format of a catalog otherwise printed to hardcopy, then to manually convert this to an online format. Most commonly this involves either manual HTML conversion, or the more laborious task of separating content, presentation format and raw data into normalized elements that can be coded in XML and dynamically published from a common repository. It is not difficult to imagine how the cost of the latter approach can reach into millions of dollars, particularly in the case of catalogs involving hundreds of thousands of products.

Failure to address this level of integration, however, would introduce a significant competitive hurdle for the commerce portal from the perspective of the potential buyer. The real value-add of the e-catalog is not the availability of information alone, but rather confidence in the ability to execute a comprehensive query from a single source. Just as engineers are incented to participate as prosumers in an info-ecology around product information, buyers participating in commerce portals are driven by a reduction in one of the most prolific transaction costs to plague the procurement process—the cost of searching.

Purchases of standard products in the offline world is accomplished by poring through catalog after catalog, or simply re-ordering out of exasperation with them. The success of a commerce portal requires delivering the confidence that any search result is going to be comprehensive and conclusive, and that the information presented is normalized in such as way as to allow a direct comparison. Failure to do this simply accelerates the aggravation of searching multiple catalogs and creates a negative feedback loop that will quickly result in the exchange's failure.

The Vertical Aggregator

The goal for most exchanges is to build market liquidity by increasing trading volume. The currency is transaction fees. Today exchanges charge transaction fees of anywhere from 0.5 percent to 10 percent on the sales executed through their systems. With exchange transaction volume expected to reach $5 to $7 trillion dollars over the next few years, it is understandable that these exchanges would be excited at the possibilities for wealth. If the 1,000 exchanges that exist today were to equally divide up just a 5 percent commission on $7 trillion, they would each earn $350 million.

It is likely that the 1,000 or 10,000 exchanges that exist a few years from now will be splitting up aggregate fees in the millions, not trillions.

But consider that in 1998, the NYSE traded volume of an aggregate value of over $7.3 trillion on over 168 billion trades, which resulted in net revenue to the exchange (transaction fees) of only $110 million. This amounts to a commission of about 0.000015 percent. This fee would have been considerably higher 20 to 30 years ago, when securities dealers became fat on large commissions with fixed minimums. But as a result of more efficient trading networks such as NASDAQ and other deregulation, the transaction fees the NYSE is able to charge have shrunk to a fraction of what they once were.

This erosion of transaction fees is inevitable for exchanges. Just as the aggregate stock market required significant reductions in transaction costs to reach the exponential growth in volume required to reach today's levels, the explosive growth expected for exchange volume will also require drastically reduced transaction costs. Transaction fees will move toward zero, following an exponential curve inverse to growth in volume. It is likely that the 1,000 or 10,000 exchanges that exist a few years from now will be splitting up aggregate fees in the millions, not trillions.

> The NYSE is the most prescient example of the inherent limitation of revenue models based on transaction fees.

In recognition of shrinking transaction fees, a new business model is emerging that seeks to be more than just the marketmaker for a select number of transactions, but the dominant platform for commercial activity across an entire industry—rather a marketplace, THE marketplace.

These businesses, called vertical aggregators, are beginning to emerge in all industries, from healthcare to food services to steel to agriculture, and will likely prove to be one of the most dynamic frontiers in the X-economy.

Most of the earliest first movers in this space originated as distributors and independent manufacturer's reps that have recognized the threat to their business model from forces such as disintermediation by manufacturers and the margin squeezing effect of the Internet in general is having on traditional distribution channels.

The migration path for these businesses typically follows a specific pattern with very little variation:

1. First seek to build communities around specific areas of interest, using vertically targeted content to build a critical mass of potential buyers.
2. Aggressively court industry kingpins on the buyer and seller side as anchor clients.
3. Go live on a trading floor with the backing of anchor clients.
4. Begin unveiling a suite of allied services, moving true end-to-end transaction capabilities.

The time to complete this cycle, from content to complete services, is shrinking quickly, while the cost is growing from a few millions to tens of millions of dollars. The stakes, however, are extremely high. While there might be room for many different exchanges within the same industry, there is room for only one dominant platform. Exchanges can be utilized on a purely opportunistic basis and represent a compliment to, rather than a replacement of an existing distribution channel. Platforms, however, by definition require subscription by the entire industry in order to function.

In this winner take all (or at least most) scenario, competition is predictably fierce. The prize goes to those who can build the community fastest. Where pure-play exchanges have little to offer until both trading capabilities and a critical mass of buyers and sellers are in place, the vertical aggregator must aggressively sell the idea of the platform the moment it is announced, in anticipation of the availability of end-to-end capabilities. Nonetheless, the time from concept to completion cannot be short enough, and, once the idea is public, the aggregator is vulnerable to any competitor that can organize faster. In this way, the initial stages of the rollout more resemble a nineteenth-century homestead land grab than a twenty-first-century exchange—each contender seeking to out-partner the other.

One of the first test cases of this business model is e-STEEL, a neutral site founded by steel executives in 1999. The e-STEEL community of trading partners is comprised of approximately 3,000 member organizations throughout 90 countries, representing service centers, fabricators, distributors, trading companies, and major OEMs.

Keeping with the sequence above, e-STEEL first went live as a community portal, comprised primarily of syndicated content on the steel industry through a partnership with Quote.com. At the same time, the company began courting the top players in the steel industry, such as USX, U.S. Steel, Cargill, and Worthington. The clear benefit of successfully organizing this type of partnership is instant liquidity. In e-STEEL's case, within hours of switching on its trading capabilities, two of its leading producers had already executed a transaction across the system.

The metals industry (in general as well as steel specifically) is defined by a dominant group of producers who sell to a much larger number of processors who further refine the product and, in turn, sell to an even larger number of distributors who deal directly with buyers. Failure to win the support of the top producers would prevent the viability of any exchange platform. For one, e-STEEL charges only the seller a fixed transaction fee of 0.875 percent with no charge to the buyer.

Another reason for signing leading suppliers early is to capitalize on the ability to support existing relationships among trading partners. Rather than focusing solely on bringing together buyers and sellers who would not otherwise find each other, the vertical aggregator must offer a layer of business infrastructure that creates value by simplifying or otherwise enhancing current business practices among vertical constituents. In this way, the vertical aggregator is competing on a different level than other exchanges, whose value proposition is more about supply chain optimization than generating liquidity by opening secondary markets.

To this end, e-STEEL's primary thrust is a set technology built specifically for trade within the steel industry called STEELDIRECT. This allows the creation of VPN (Virtual Private Network) capability for existing trading communities to participate within the e-STEEL framework, but without radically alternating existing practices. For example, those partners that have existing contracts in place can manage them through this network without adversely affecting production runs, while also participating in the e-STEEL exchange for extracting volume from excess capacity or picking price advantages on spot buys.

e-STEEL has also produced deeper integration technology through partners such as webMethods. These include a proprietary technology called DATAJET that is used for integrating with legacy systems for managing steel product information and catalogs, as well as a variant of XML called SML or Steel Mark-up Language that serves as a common intermediary for linking various systems among the members of the e-STEEL community.

These services offer the value-added capability of supply chain optimization and access to allied services such as collaborative development and logistics management, and are at the heart of the vertical aggregator business model. Specifically, the sustainable vertical aggregator organization will build value and derive revenue through access to verticalized solutions. Long term this will lead to the erosion of transaction fees (which for e-STEEL are already less than 1 percent).

A caveat carried with these additional capabilities, however, is that the vertical aggregator faces a challenge not encountered by most other exchange models and dot-com organizations—selling enterprise-level applications. Despite initial development phases that resemble those of any content-oriented Internet portal, vertical aggregators are evolving in a direction that more closely resembles the direction of software vendors.

In this way, the vertical aggregator platform is emerging as a hybrid form of next generation ERP and EDI. This has not gone without detection by the software industry, notably ERP players such as Oracle and SAP. The business of enterprise software applications is notably different from hosting exchanges on the Internet. The challenge to vertical aggregators is for each to develop this capacity, before being usurped by existing ERP players moving toward this type of offering from the other direction. Of critical importance to vertical aggregators will be lining up the right partners, capable of handling the unique nuances and sophistication involved in the sale and execution of enterprise and interenterprise applications.

Favoring the vertical aggregators, however, is that the ERP players are behind in rallying a community in the way the e-STEEL and others have. The test will be whether community support or existing market penetration of internal infrastructure proves the more dominant force.

The Infomediary

To date the vast majority of exchanges have focused on content (vis-à-vis the electronic billboard), often combining industry-related news with virtual community capabilities such as discussion forums.

For businesses looking to establish an online presence from the ground-up, content and community are the easiest and least expensive to deliver and fastest to rollout, and are used both to lure potential trading partners and to begin building mind-share for the exchange. While this type of offering can be a key leverage point for building the community, the ability to translate this into a sustainable business model is limited.

The next stage is the opening of the trading floor, involving the deployment of basic commerce capabilities, such as the opportunity to check product availability, post orders, and ultimately complete the commercial exchange. This transition from content provider to that of an actual exchange is critical to the business' evolution, as it provides a direct revenue stream, typically as a percentage of transaction revenue.

The migration path is away from selling off-the-shelf products to managing increasingly complex transactions and facilitating commerce and collaboration among multiple community members. As illustrated in Figure 3.6, the movement is toward exchanges that focus on generating trading efficiency among increasingly complex products and services.

Emerging from this trend are two new business models which, when executed properly, offer far greater levels of sustainability and realization of value. These represent the instantiation of the N:N community model described earlier in the section on Metcalfe's Law and increasing returns theory.

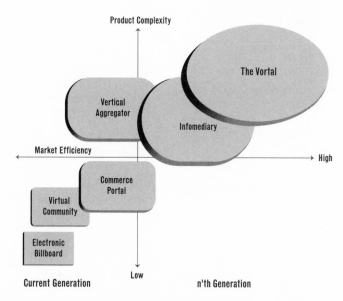

Figure 3.6   The path of exchange evolution is toward the ability to serve increasingly complex buyer demands with higher levels of efficiency.

The first, called the *Infomediary,* starts with a customer base initially, then leverages the aggregated purchasing power of the community to bargain with suppliers and service providers.[2] The second is a newly emerging business model called the Vortal, that transcends the transaction-oriented perspective of previous models and enables multidimensional, end-to-end completion of an entire value-chain cycle—from collaborative design to collaborative production to negotiated commerce to the management of fulfillment and logistics.

The basis of the infomediary is the notion of horizontal market integration or, as it's sometimes referred to, *value bundling.* To appreciate the potential power of this model, consider for a moment your own commercial relationships—once a business has invested the time and attention to capture your trust and to smooth the process of

---

[2] The term *infomediary* is credited to John Hagel and Marc Singer, authors of *Net Worth,* January 1999, Harvard Business School.

doing business with them, would you rather buy peripheral products and services from them or go through the trouble of evaluating an entirely new source? For most the answer comes with little hesitation—across all industries buyers look for single source purchase options.

For very large organizations, mundane purchases such as office supplies and long distance service may represent substantial sources of expense and as such warrant careful scrutiny and management. For the other 90 percent of business buyers, however, these rarely command the average manager's time. Most businesses do not have the time to haggle over the best price for all purchases, particularly for nonstrategic products and services, purchases typically follow the path of least resistance. But as U.S. Senator Everett Dirksen once remarked in the middle of a debate over the federal budget, "A million here, and a million there, and pretty soon you're talking about real money." When a community of organizations look at their combined spending, it is clear that seemingly innocuous purchases add up to real money.

For buyers, the value proposition of the infomediary is to redirect the path of least resistance by reducing transaction costs associated with sourcing products and negotiating with sellers. Although competitive prices are an implicit benefit of the infomediary, the true clincher for buyers is being the most convenient alternative to do business with. To achieve this, it employs the tactics of the previously mentioned models: providing relevant real-time information, offering a community of users as a reference base for purchasing decisions, automating back-end processes such as order fulfillment, inventory management, and distribution, and offering a collaborative portal environment enabling personalized interaction.

It is important to note, however, that the value proposition of the infomediary is not lopsided in favor of buyers. Although buyers clearly benefit, the same dynamics create value for sellers through the presence of an existing group of buyers bound by trust-based relationships, as well as access to valuable proprietary information about current and future market needs.

The combination of these elements creates a positive feedback loop where the prospect of a lucrative base of buyers leads to the addition of new sellers, presenting a new set of opportunities that attracts new buyers to the community, thus in turn increasing the value offered to sellers. Once the infomediary sets this momentum into motion, a power dynamic of increasing returns sets in, creating a self-sustaining market where the barriers to entry by outside competitors are extraordinarily high.

The infomediary faces one of the steepest curves in the time-to-community cycle. Once critical mass is reached, the model grows at an extraordinarily fast rate. Getting to this point, however, is not half the battle—it is *the* battle. The challenge of building this community is largely cultural, focused around the issue of trust, which we examine in detail in Chapter 4.

The Vortals: Collaborative Communities of Commerce

As we have discussed throughout this book, transaction costs are rapidly shrinking. These are not the toll charges for participation in an exchange, but rather the operational costs of coordinating value chain activities. This has shifted the source of competitive advantage from proprietary ownership of vertically integrated infrastructure to liquid value chains built from *disintegrated* molecular components. This shift has also created an *infrastructure void,* requiring a new open platform for industrywide collaboration. Vortals are a type of exchange that fill this void.

Vortals add a third dimension to the exchange equation. While other models approach the market from either vertical depth or horizontal breadth, each remains comparatively transaction-oriented in nature. Vortals, by contrast, extend this perspective by taking each transaction and coordinating the entire value chain of activities that support and surround it.

Think of the N:N communities previously described, but not as a flat, two-dimensional matrix. Instead, picture three dimensions with matrixes stacked upon matrixes, each one representing a specific line of business or area of collaboration, such as product design, production forecasting, distribution logistics, commercial financing, and so on.

> Vortals represent a major power shift, where market domi-
> nance is no longer based on proprietary access to resources,
> but rather the ability to coordinate an entire value chain, from
> product planning through development, manufacturing, sales,
> and distribution.

Vortals represent a major power shift, where market dominance is no longer based on proprietary access to resources, but rather the ability to coordinate an entire value chain, from product planning through development, manufacturing, sales, and distribution.

The majority of business conducted through exchanges in the near term will not be about bringing together buyers and sellers who would not otherwise work together (although this is clearly were the long-term opportunity is), but rather will be done among trusted, well-established partners. The tools needed by these participants are those that empower these relationships, not those designed to replace them. This translates to the need for an open, Web-based platform which enables business collaboration, builds on the strength of existing relationships, and reduces indecision during the negotiation process by presenting all relevant information within a mutually accessible, single point of access.

Forget the traditional conventions of the marketplace where buyers and sellers meet at the point where a need and resource have been identified without regard to the surrounding activities. Vortals support an awareness of industry and business activity, such as anticipating parts shortages based on other orders and involving suppliers in product development on a real-time basis. Vortals are therefore in essence the platform for all areas of business activity, not merely a meeting place for transacting a sale.

For example, one layer of the vortal supports the collaborative activities surrounding the bid for a product. Once it has been negotiated and accepted between a buyer and seller, however, financing, shipping, and insurance is required. Prior to this stage, production must be scheduled, raw materials must be ordered, delivery must be scheduled. Traditionally, each one of these processes is managed as discrete activity.

Value-Chain Linkages

While logical linkages exist across the entire value chain, as we previously examined, physical linkages are likely limited to point-to-point connections, if they exist at all. This is because the tools traditionally applied to these processes are designed for discrete, hardwired transactions. Tools such as EDI, supply-chain management, product configuration, and ERP are not collaborative in nature but rather very task specific.

Vortals offer a collaborative platform to connect all of the necessary elements of these environments with all participants across the value chain, at the moment they need it. It would be impractical and self-defeating to provide, for example, all participants in a value chain access to each other's ERP or product data management systems. Each of these, however, contain critical information necessary to fulfilling a complete transaction. Vortals base their incremental value-added on delivering just such services in ways that fit with participants' existing business requirements.

One of the first areas vortals address is that of collaborative sourcing and planning. For instance, if I am going to buy from you I need to know what you have on hand for inventory and when you can produce what I want. This requires integration with the back-end systems (inventory, production, fulfillment) of the various parties involved, but it also mandates honest disclosure about availability of resources. For most organizations, even long time partners, this represents a major cultural shift. Few organizations are accustomed to this level of exposure and are instead preconditioned to say "sure we got that" when they really mean "I'm sure we can get that."

The absence of this level of disclosure results in dangerous delays in responsiveness and indecision. In the real-time environment of the X-economy, organizations no longer have the luxury of pushing selected information to value-chain constituents. All community members must have the ability to pull information from a wide range of applications and resources spread across the value chain. This means an entirely new level of trust among partners, but it also requires an unprecedented level of connectivity. This is a fundamental infrastructure requirement of vortals.

From Portals to Vortals

An important point of distinction between vortals and the portal interfaces of many existing exchanges revolves around who holds the reins controlling content. While a typical portal may provide some degree of personalization, it likely does not allow a large degree of flexibility with regards to information not predetermined by the exchange administrator. Decisions and negotiations require more than content such as news feeds and stock quotes. Required is support for the inclusion of design specifications; contracts and other bidding documents; the capture of e-mail conversations; links to information sources outside of the exchange environment; and a variety of other ad hoc documents that are otherwise faxed and FedEx'd back and forth during the normal process of business-to-business negotiations.

While the first generation of exchanges typically relied on historic content, such as product data and industry news, this is often of little use to partners engaged in an active decision process. Vortals shift the control of content from the administrator to individual participants in a collaborative process. The challenge has been, however, that content management tools are designed to serve-up information from specifically structured repositories, not to allow individuals to assemble content on their own.

Vortals enable partners to create a private workplace within an exchange, allowing individual management of information simultaneously with a centralized single point of collaboration. This provides support of the closed-loop, reciprocal processes involved with collaboration, such as the development of requirements definition, validation of designs, and specifications and negotiation of terms and conditions. This allows collaborating sellers to increase buyer confidence by facilitating the verification of capabilities, the demonstration of competencies, and the validation of references.

Another aspect of collaboration is the ability to facilitate the selling of concepts and ideas internally. With a typical exchange, little consideration is given to the need of buyers to find sponsors for a project or product. Once the terms have been negotiated with various selling constituents, the buyer would have little to show as history and other supporting information. Vortals encapsulate the information within an environment easily navigated by management, legal counsel, or other participants brought into the decision process during the later stages of collaboration. This same capability extends to post-sales processes, such as facilitating the transfer of knowledge about product use and implementation, selecting and coordinating partners for integration and other aftermarket activities.

Complexity and Efficiency

By supporting each activity in the business process, from collaborative design to production, vortals maximize the two otherwise diametrically opposed elements of value creation—complexity and efficiency. The antithesis of standardization, complexity represents the delta between what a buyer wants and what the market has to offer in its basic, nonvalued elements. Standardized products typically offered the benefit of efficiency (translated into reduced cost and increased availability), yet come at the expense of a one-size-fits-all proposition.

In most cases, buyers must make economic trade-offs between complexity and efficiency. In the case of products such as software, buyers may chose a product that meets 70 percent of their requirements, then pay a premium to account for the difference (although likely less than 30 percent) through custom programming and integration services. In the case of manufactured products, the difficulty in bridging this gap may be considerably more difficult and come at a much higher cost.

By enabling organizations to efficiently collaborate with a much tighter degree of intimacy, vortals enable the value chain to organize around each opportunity, providing the optimal composition of resources necessary to most closely match each individual customer's desires. This is at the heart of Paul Romer's new growth theory, enabling the members of collaborative communities of commerce to reassemble a finite number of resources into a virtually unlimited number of new product recipes.

This Vortal Coil

While significant steps forward have already been taken in the direction of vortals, realizing the full potential of this model requires clearing some significant technical and cultural hurdles. The former is most easily solved, and indeed where most advances are being made today.

Vertical aggregators are the furthest along with end-to-end capabilities and could be the first to complete the transition from commerce platform to true hub for collaboration across the value chain. Collaborative planning capabilities and various other tools for value-chain optimization are already in place with aggregators such as Inc2Inc. In tandem with this, other aggregators are moving ahead with capabilities around collaborative design and project management. Although none has yet to offer a truly comprehensive solution, the degree of M&A activity in the vertical aggregator space is helping to quickly evolve the capabilities of this segment. If and when the inflection point occurs however, it is likely to be clouded by competing interests among private consortia and buyer-owned procurement sites, such as Covisint. As illustrated in Figure 3.7, there are multiple paths towards the realization of the vortal model.

What other contenders lack is the leverage held by buyer-managed commerce portals such as Covisint. These exchanges are where the 800-pound gorilla is in the driver's seat, not in the backseat or as some aggregators have found, standing in the middle of the road. Working in their favor, however, is that gorillas can't drive.

Compared with the aggregators, buyer-managed markets such as Covisint are, by definition, completely self-serving, focused more on operational efficiency than opportunity creation, and slow to move. They also have the disadvantage of scrutiny from regulatory bodies—something the more innocuous smaller players have largely avoided. Although they have received initial clearance, they remain under the watchful eye of the FTC, and as such must go to great lengths to avoid the appearance of collusion. As a result, Covisint may be less likely to proceed with some of the more intimate areas of collaboration required to truly instantiate the vortal model.

Whoever takes the lead, it is not difficult to imagine how this new breed of power brokers could easily wield more clout than the

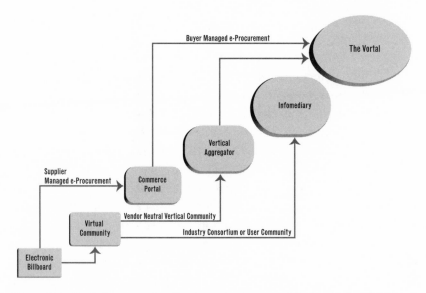

Figure 3.7   Evolutionary paths of exchange business models flow in the direction of increasing business complexity and stronger bonds between community members.

largest of today's organizations—perhaps even leading to an entirely new kind of monopolistic phenomenon. The economic ramifications are incredible to imagine. Whether manufacturer, distributor, or customer, the question is not whether they will redefine your business model, but how quickly you will react and what path you will take.

A significant aspect of this is the ability to tap into core competency service providers with the same degree of interchangeability as any other community participant. In order to fill the gaps within the collective capabilities of the community, or simply to outsource services peripheral to the core focus of community members, a new opportunity has emerged in the form of online services targeting discrete points along the value chain. This new breed of service provider presents the packaging of business expertise and software in a single-point-of-access for vortals and other exchange models.

Business Service Providers

In the late 1970s, John Cullinane, founder of what later became the industry's pioneering applications vendor, Cullinet Corporation, was the first person to suggest the possibility of packaged applications that would embody the collective knowledge of many experts into off-the-shelf application programs. He was considered foolish by most, and outright insane by everyone else. Yet the Cullinane model became the standard for applications packaging during the last two decades. Accountants, engineers, marketing professionals, sales personnel, and virtually anyone else looking at new applications would not think twice about using an off-the-shelf or one-off (i.e., a slightly customized) software application over a customized application designed and built from ground zero. That metaphor is now on the verge of changing again—just as radically as it did 30 years ago—with the advent of what has been called the ASP model.

Application Service Providers (ASPs) offer the equivalent of applications on loan. Simply put, they give you the option of using applications as you need them rather than purchasing expensive software. The applications and, in some cases, the data are hosted on a remote computer. Using an ASP, expensive and complex applications such as databases, enterprise resource planning, customer relationship management, and sales automation solutions can be hosted on a third-party computer and leased by user organizations.

With the creation of ASP environments, users will no longer see, or even care about, discrete applications such as these or even standard applications such as word processing processors or spreadsheets; instead they will work within a hosted portal that stitches together the various component technologies and information sources they need to accomplish a particular task.

Those bearish on the ASP model enjoy pointing to the drawn-out failure of Pandesic, one of the early ASPs, in support of their argument. This joint venture by SAP and Intel had established the benchmark for the ASP business model in 1997, but today is the poster child for ASP naysayers convinced the model can never work. And it may not, for those who have built their value proposition around cost savings. The fact is that any out-sourced business model that focuses entirely on cost-savings is doomed from the start. Organizations do not outsource to save money, they outsource to gain expertise.

Many ASPs are chasing traditional outsourcing vendors in the hope of reviving their sputtering businesses. Their pitch is virtually identical to what their partners have used for the last 30 years—reducing the total cost of ownership for enterprise applications. The problem is, no one is buying it. Despite great aspirations, the market they serve today is largely comprised of low-margin Web site hosting, not mission-critical applications. A recent survey by Delphi Group of over 1,000 major organizations showed that less than 15 percent had any expectations of using an ASP to host enterprise applications.

While the current herd of ASPs struggle with the outsourcing business model, a new breed of service provider has emerged which combines software subscription capabilities with deeply embedded vertical knowledge.

Business Service Providers (BSPs) are emerging as the central hubs for hosting collaboration within exchanges. These e-service providers offer a bundle of highly verticalized proprietary software with specific community-oriented domain knowledge, collaborative capabilities, and embedded business processes.

Rather than hosting horizontal applications for organizations on an individual basis, BSPs provide the computing platform for an entire vertical community. Emerging within industries ranging from construction to commercial finance, these BSPs provide a critical set of services to each vertical community.

Where the Cullinane model serves as the application prototype of the BSP, Automated Data Processing (ADP) is its business role model. ADP has built an empire around the seemingly mundane task of payroll management. In the process it has demonstrated the value outsourcing processes peripheral to most organization's core competency. Through a network of BSP partners, ADP offers exchanges the opportunity to provide its members with not only payroll services, but management of travel and expense accounting, human resource benefits management, and other employee-related services.

Another BSP is Escrow.com who offers exchanges a verity of transaction management services. As with other BSP models, Escrow.com offers Web-delivered software services with embedded process knowledge surrounding transaction and financial risk management such as escrow services and international letters of credit. Like ADP, Escrow.com delivers this with a network of services partners.

Underlying the BSP model is a concept that offers a redefinition of traditional enterprise computing, one which takes an inside-out perspective of connecting with community partners rather than the inward-facing view of locally deployed applications, what we call a Business Operating System (BOS).

The BOS is a process-based environment that encapsulates the unique knowledge of how a business is run and the way people and information come together to add value to a business process within a specific trading community. From an architectural perspective, the BOS consists of a common operating environment (read Java) and business process library, expressed through a consistent standardized Web-based environment.

Why is this so radical? Because it represents a level of process integration heretofore unknown. Think of the simplicity and process transparency of an online service such as ADP's payroll outsourcing, then apply this notion to all the touch points across your value chain. That is the BOS—rather than simply presenting a Web interface to specific applications, with no explicit continuity among process participants, this new breed of ASP exists as the business process itself.

The heart of the BSP is the BOS. Layered on top of it are the business processes and business knowledge that define each BSP's unique differentiation. BSPs online today have deployed the BOS concept in fairly narrow slices, offering software and services first around discrete processes, such as bid development, then loosely coupling them to related areas which involve the same participants, for example project management.

This hub orientation of the BSP presents an obvious benefit here, allowing organizations to share centralized information from process to process. But it also points to the role of BSPs as service aggregators, leveraging this information to provide additional value-added services.

The BSP which hosts the process and information for developing a bid between collaborating suppliers can utilize the same centralized data to generate a unified bill of materials, or generate compliance documentation incorporating each participant's specific data. Both of these are likely requirements of a collaborative bid and are particularly resource-intensive in the absence of a centralized facilitator.

Why will the BSP succeed where ASPs have failed? Because the BSP model is community-based, rather than application-centric, it benefits from the dynamic of increasing returns. The more organizations within the community that use it the more valuable it becomes to all participants. This latter concept of community-driven value and "prosumers" is further developed in Chapter 5. What is critical to BSPs, however, is an organic growth capability allowing them to grow exponentially, easily outpacing the growth path of the traditional ASP.

Takeaways

The discussion in this chapter covered how the principles of Metcalfe's Law are being addressed by today's X-economy business models. New e-businesses such as exchanges, portals, vertical aggregators, and other similar ground-breaking paradigms have emerged as businesses try to address the fragmentation of markets by implementing technologies and mechanisms that help build and foster *communities.*

The business models covered and the technologies that enable them included:

Bidirectional Exchanges

Electronic Auctions

Electronic Billboards

Virtual Communities

Commerce Portals

Vertical Aggregators

Infomediaries

Vortals

Business Service Providers

In each case, the fundamental principle behind each business model is to create specialized communities for their respective markets, closely addressing the needs of their customer base. Recognizing that "business" frequently extends beyond the primary organization's four walls, these business models address the extended community, linking the entire value chain to increased awareness and responsiveness, thereby maximizing the ability to recognize and react to changes in the market—gaining the most leverage from the investment of time.

Business Service Providers are emerging in the market as another answer to the question of how to maximize return on time (ROT) by providing complete infrastructure solutions, including IT resources, applications, and business processes, specifically addressed to distinct lines of businesses.

CHAPTER 4

Rule 3:
The X-Economy
Is Built on Trust
Not Transactions

Every kind of peaceful cooperation among men is primarily based on mutual trust and only secondarily on institutions such as courts of justice and police.

Albert Einstein

When the enormous infrastructure of the cable industry was being created, the greatest hurdle to overcome was that of connecting the cable to the millions of consumers who formed the final link in realizing the value of cable. This incredible undertaking came to be known in the cable and telecommunications industry as the "the Last Mile problem." The Last Mile is a classic case of building infrastructure for any massive connectivity scenario. Shipping, oil and gas, and retail distribution all suffer from the same phenomenon: Namely, you have to build the entirety of an infrastructure before you can capitalize on the benefits of delivering even a single ounce of product to the market.

For the X-economy, the Last Mile is not the network's band-width, computer desktops, or even the standards for networking and communications, all of which are well evolved to facilitate most all enterprise transactions. Instead, it is the very real and often dis-counted factor of trust.

It was Adam Smith who popularized the notion of an unforeseen hand that shapes markets by creating commerce in light of and despite the selfish interests of its participants. What Smith could not have fore-seen was the complexity of conflicting interests that would be involved in establishing the modern marketplace. It is in this cauldron of con-flicting interests that Smith's invisible hand becomes a tangible reality.

As ethereal and fuzzy as the concept may be, trust creates a very real and insurmountable impediment to forming the sorts of partner-ships necessary for the X-economy to take off. Creating marketplaces that engender trust involves overcoming many separate problems in the formation of both the transactions and the relationships.

In many cases, it is the intangible elements of a relationship that provides the security to consummate a transaction. These are the sorts of courtesies and gestures such as luxury box seats to a sporting event, or lunch or dinner that build a relationship between business partners.

But what is not often considered is the way in which trust needs to be established in complex multipartner transactions. Take for example the real estate industry where the role of fiduciaries has become essen-tial to establishing the trust necessary to conduct a transaction be-tween anonymous parties.

This is a prime example of how trust can be brokered and bartered by a third party. Lawyers, escrow agents, and brokers are all put in a position of creating trust between parties who otherwise have every reason to look out for their own best interests, thereby creating a lack of trust.

If you apply these same concepts to an online marketplace, some interesting conclusions arise. First, as value chains accelerate, they cre-ate greater volatility in partnerships and alliances. Value chains reform repeatedly as partners recombine competencies to construct new products and services. This results in increasingly less time available to form trust-based relationships. Ultimately, this is the governor that limits growth of the X-economy.

But these are not new issues. Trust has always been a limiting factor, which is why the legal profession is one of the largest beneficiaries of any economic boom. As economic and social institutions accelerate, we supplant the inability to form bonds of trust in a one-to-one modality with fiduciary relationships. These fiduciaries become the clearinghouse for trust by being the points of stability in an otherwise transient set of relationships.

But let's go even further out on a limb. If the nature of the relationships formed in the X-economy is by definition increasingly more transient, then trust becomes harder and harder to come by in business partnerships. If for no other reason than this, exchanges become the only place of permanence for trust, becoming the binding factor in forming a fast and malleable economy.

Trust and the N:N Marketplace

In our discussion of the X-economy framework, one of our conclusions is that the fundamental relationship between supply chain and demand chain was that in the demand chain model (the upper right-hand quadrant of the X-economy framework) relationships between supply and demand occur in a recombinant fashion. An interesting twist on this model is to consider what it means for this relationship in a historical context.

If we travel back to Henry Ford's assembly line model, the relationship between supply and demand chain was a simple 1:N model where a single product (one shape, size, color) satisfied the needs of many consumers. The same applied to business transactions where every member of a supply chain had to produce products and services that would conform to standardized processes. This was the great revolution of manufacturing that was popularized in the mass production of small arms. But it created a legacy that shaped the entirety of not only the supply chain but also the modern marketplace.

The modern value chain is still very much like the Minoan palace, with corridors that wind and turn in myriad directions. Specialization and highly distributed operations have created monstrously complex interactions between enterprises. The walls we have placed between the parts of an organization, its people, suppliers, customers, and all participants of the value chain are artificial. Michael Porter has said, "Organizational structure in most firms works against achieving interrelationships."[1] We would go further to say that the very structure of value chains works against achieving interrelationships among enterprises.

> The entire supply chain must work together in limitless combination to meet the needs of limitless requirements of the demand chain. This is the essence of what may be the greatest revolution yet in how we view partnerships.

The end to the tyranny of the supply chain was seen by many to be mass customization; the process of running a mass manufacturing assembly line that produced effective quantities of one for each customer's requirements. But mass customization is at best a one-to-one model (think back to our X-economy framework and the center of the quadrants where the X and Y axes intersect). Mass customization ignores the very real problems associated with rebuilding a supply chain that provides the many components necessary for a new product. In fact, the least likely scenario in most manufacturing processes is that a modification results in only one component being changed.

This many-to-many (or N:N) situation can best be termed mass collaboration, where the entire supply chain must work together in limitless combinations to meet the needs of limitless requirements of the demand chain.

---

[1] Porter, Michael E. *Competitive Advantage: Creating and Sustaining Superior Performance* (New York: Free Press, p. 365, 1998).

This is the essence of what may be the greatest revolution yet in how we view partnerships not only within the supply chain, but also among supply and demand chains.

The best example of this is the now infamous Napster. Napster is an utterly simple concept. Acting as an online matching service, it connects individuals who are seeking pieces of music by specific performers with other individuals who have the music resident on their computers. Napster never takes possession of the music. The music only resides on the computers of the parties involved in the transaction.

Napster has introduced into our vernacular the idea of peer-to-peer, or P2P, communications. P2P brings the issue of trust to center stage in a way that epitomizes the sort of complex challenges businesses will face in the coming years.

The idea is not complex: Allow computers to talk to each other and share files directly without having to go through an intermediary. What makes this interesting is that it flies in the face of what appears to be the obvious place of residence for trust in the X-economy, the exchange. This apparent contradiction is not easily resolved.

What is clear is that the Napster P2P model is the most viral approach to date for creating connections. In terms of the number of users, it is the fastest growing Web site in history, with over 25 million in its first year! But, Napster has gained much more notoriety for the copyright issues that P2P involves. However, these have eclipsed the purpose that Shawn Fanning, its creator, had when he first conceived of Napster.

Fanning was driven by a vision of a community that could share music without a middleman. It is no different than what any one of us has done dozens of times by recording our favorite music to cassette tapes and then sharing the tapes with friends. It's just that now the friends were an anonymous global community, nameless faces—each of which has a very specific need or just as specific an offer. Each use of Napster was still a 1:1 relationship between individuals but the number of possible 1:1 relationships was unlimited (well, actually 62,500,000,000,000,000).

In the case of sharing music for free, the issue of trust is rather insignificant. If the song you get isn't what you had hoped for, you have lost little but a few minutes of time. If we move up to consumer applications, such as eBay, trust becomes somewhat more of an issue. Minimally, trust needs to be engendered by the brand's reputation. However, if we apply the idea of P2P to business exchanges, trust becomes a significant factor since considerable value, services, and products are being exchanged with an effect that trickles down through the entire value chain.

It is difficult today to conceive of this sort of networked, peer-based economy as having integrity. In fact, many private exchanges openly acknowledge that their real value is not in building trust but rather in simply facilitating current transactions between existing partners.

But think for a moment about the issue of scaling these exchanges to reach larger numbers of buyers and sellers—what we have already called the function of liquidity. Napster would never work if it did not operate in the face of enormous anonymity. At the heart of this type of anonymous market is the idea of an exchange that at the very least validates that the items being exchanged between peers conform to some basic level of preestablished guidelines. In the case of Napster, this means creating a master search index that verifies the existence of a file (music) on one computer that has been requested by another computer.

In the case of Napster, the role of the exchange is slim, a sophisticated matching service. The onus for performance is on the individuals. But what about an exchange that deals in real estate, machine parts for airliners, medical devices, or other such critical and complex transactions? In a P2P network who establishes and validates the criteria for performance? Who enforces them?

While trust seems to be an issue of emotion and intuition (i.e., someone has a trustworthy character or demeanor) it is also a precept of commerce. As such, what we often fail to recognize is that trust is structural, not just intellectual. In other words, trust has been legislated, documented, proceduralized, and incorporated into the very bedrock of commerce in tangible ways.

Consider, for example, the last time you bought a house or a car requiring the involvement of a third-party lending institution. Chances are good that you did not have a personal relationship with the banker, the real estate broker, the underwriters, the escrow agents, the appraisers, or even the seller. Yet you all established a sense of trust with each other by adhering to certain basic tenets of performance. These were not rules that anyone came up with for your particular transaction. They are rules that take concrete form in the myriad documents, laws, contracts, procedures, and regulations governing the transaction.

Without these structural aspects of trust in place, far fewer homes would be bought and sold. Structural trust is, in fact, a method of creating liquidity by decreasing the level of uncertainty inherent in dealing with otherwise anonymous parties.

But what often slows down complex transactions that rely on this sort of trust is the one-off or slightly customized modifications that need to be made to the many structural pieces of the transaction intended to provide for trustworthy performance. This is especially true when new business partners, suppliers, buyers, or any new party enters the community of trade. In a perverse way, the very mechanism that creates more liquidity is the culprit in stifling even greater liquidity.

In an N:N market, this presents a significant impediment since the potential partners are largely anonymous.

What if it were possible to incorporate not only the structural elements of trust into an exchange, but to go even further to allow for their instant modification to meet the needs of new participants? Effectively this type of exchange would provide trust by validating the identity of participants, validating the competencies of participants, and enforcing the performance expectations of the participants.

This is not a pipe dream. Exchanges such as AltraEnergy.com (a leading player in the brokering of energy products such as oil, gas, and electric power) are already either building these sorts of mechanisms into their foundation while others are relying on a third party—Trust Service Providers (TSPs) such as escrow.com—to deliver this.

In the case of another exchange, GoFish.com, their trust element came in the form of one of their strongest value propositions: a proprietary credit database that the parent company, Seafax, had developed. Since 1985, Seafax had been serving the seafood community by collecting and providing credit information and history on merchants in the market. At the time of GoFish.com's release, this database consisted of over 1,100 customers and they had a deep understanding of how their buyers and sellers interacted. The GoFish exchange provides both buyers and sellers with an online ability to conduct commerce globally and efficiently by matching buyers' needs with sellers' inventories. However, the strength in the GoFish model went far beyond a simple matching capability; because these buyers and sellers, through GoFish, were part of the Seafax family, a seller received a Seafax report with the buyer's order, assuring the seller of the buyer's credit-worthiness before the transaction took place. Because of the backing of Seafax, sellers can trust that they will be paid for their goods.

GoFish can take this level of trust one step further. In conjunction with one of the largest credit insurers in the world, GoFish provides to their sellers an additional security net. If, for some reason, the buyer is unable to pay—due to catastrophic loss of the business before the payment is issued, for example—the credit insurer guarantees the payment to the seller. So GoFish exchange members can trust that their transaction is not at risk.

In each of these cases and many others, trust has become part of the structural architecture of the exchange. Yet, it is just as important for these exchanges to provide a strong element of infomediation, which we introduced in the last chapter, as a vehicle by which to preserve the trust already in place among closely aligned communities of trade.

With an infomediary (we briefly introduced infomediaries in Chapter 3) in place, existing bonds of trust can be leveraged and expanded along with the opportunity for trade in a market.

Leveraging Trust

Without question, one of (if not the) greatest assets of an organization is customer data—buying patterns, transaction histories, packing preferences, and other pertinent data, often available only to those trusted few that have taken the time to develop and hone a relationship with the party in question.

Yet in a business atmosphere increasingly unforgiving of confidentiality compromises, organizations seeking to leverage this asset are faced with a fundamental question: How do we capitalize on customer and partner data without breaching our fiduciary responsibility to protect their privacy? In other words, how do we broker trust?

The answer lies in both a pragmatic understanding of business behavior and the strategic use of technology. For obvious reasons, businesses most often care less about being targets of unsolicited sales calls than they do about risking the exposure of proprietary information. Resolving the former is often a matter of simply establishing reciprocity—offering something of value in return for access to the buyer's information.

Establishing and maintaining the level of trust necessary to translate this information into realizable value, however, requires an entirely new approach to marketing. The term *trust* may seem to be anachronistic but it is the foundation of business valuations based on the lifetime value of customers. And although many companies pay lip service to this concept, you have to wonder if anyone really knows what the value of a lifetime relationship might be. In that context, perhaps we will someday look back at even the most absurd initial valuations of some small segment of X-economy companies as being amazingly conservative—as difficult as that may seem to appear in the past dot.com era.

But if we take a closer look at the evolution of the X-economy, it quickly becomes clear that the persistence of the relationship with the customer/partner and the value of the relationship increase dramatically as we move toward a trust-based model.

Consider the vertical aggregator model (described in Chapter 3), which is limited by the ability to grow the base of buyers without a pool of existing relationships. While it might be successful in signing on the support of leading sellers, this does little to incent buyers to hand over the intimate details about their business and trading practices. Thus, this model is fundamentally limited as a provider of neutral infrastructure rather than serving as the trusted intermediary. Until a critical mass of transactions is executed within the vertical aggregator's site, it will not likely have a window into buyer preferences and practices. This critical information, ultimately necessary to the sustainability of the business, can only be acquired through a history of transactions. Until then, the vertical aggregator is at the mercy of suppliers to generate business.

This puts the vertical aggregator at a fundamental disadvantage: Once a market has been identified, aggregators are vulnerable to competitive exchanges that are sooner able to assemble the necessary mix of constituencies. This underscores the issue of first mover advantage and the role it plays in the dynamics of increasing returns. The aggregator with the largest seller network will be able to offer the greatest number of options and most competitive pricing, thereby attracting the largest number of buyers, and, as a result, increasing their bargaining leverage over sellers. This phenomenon of increasing returns illustrates the significant competitive advantage for the aggregators that are first to cultivate a critical mass of loyal buyers and sellers. It also illustrates the potential for a business model based on the transformation into an exchange by leveraging an existing base of relationships.

The role of the market maker, or any infomediary, is simply to ensure that participants are comfortable and confident in the process.

Trust is the critical element enabling organizations to transform into a viable exchange. Organizations with fiduciary client relationships already in place gather a wealth of information about buying patterns, business goals, and other important matters over time. This presents a tremendous competitive advantage over organizations seeking to build this model from scratch, as well as those with legacy transaction data, but they have yet to gain the full trust and confidence of the buyer community.

An example of this in a very practical setting is the use of marketmakers at Free Markets, the exchange we profiled in Chapter 3 under the discussion of monopsonies. Marketmakers are individuals who coordinate the bidding activity for an auction. A marketmaker may actually be involved in finding suppliers and bidders, contacting them via fax or phone (whatever technology is available will do) to prep them for an auction and then actually holding the hand of a new bidder as they step through the sometimes anxious process of participating in an auction. As one market maker told us during one rather fast-paced auction, a bidder ended up bidding against themselves. When the marketmaker told them that it was their bid they just raised the frenetic response was, "We just want to make sure we win the auction." In these sorts of high velocity markets, there is ample room for miscommunication and mistrust. The role of the marketmaker, or any infomediary, is simply to ensure that participants are comfortable and confident in the process.

Over time, however, that role takes on the added responsibility of maintaining integrity in a process about which the infomediary increasingly has not only experience but large amounts of accumulated data. This is data that profiles the behaviors, transactions, clients, suppliers, and myriad vital signs of an exchange participant.

In the early stages of deployment, before a critical mass of relationships has been formed, achieving the necessary degree of trust is largely a function of technology. Playing on the old proverb, "trust only those whom you do not need to," the infomediary deploys a portal environment where the buyers are able to manage and monitor the custodial relationship over their own information. To fully realize the value of this model, however, this environment must also allow the infomediary to arbitrate the buyer/seller relationship by consolidating information from the community of buyers and offering this to multiple suppliers, as Figure 4.1 depicts.

Once these capabilities are in place, the advantage the infomediary holds over the previously defined models is the ability to extend horizontally into new product and service offerings. The nature of the vertical aggregator is to build its community by focusing on one specific industry vertical, such as electronic components, which inherently restricts the universe of potential buyers and sellers. In contrast, by beginning with a core community of buyers who have entrusted them with its purchasing needs, infomediaries are able to capitalize on a much greater number of revenue streams.

This subtle yet significant difference affords the infomediary model much greater scalability and extensibility and makes it a necessary part of every successful exchange.

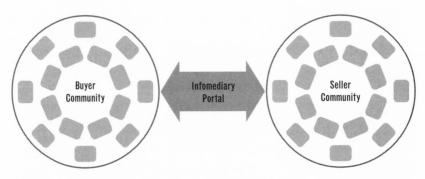

Figure 4.1   Infomediaries connect a community of buyers with a community of sellers. Following the network model of N:N communities, the value of the infomediary grows exponentially with each new member.

The New Business Culture

And when they exchange with one another, giving or receiving as the case may be, does each think that such exchange is to his own good?

Plato's Republic

So far our discussion of trust has focused on the way in which technology has altered the way companies do business, but clearly this discussion would not be complete without a look at how the X-economy affects the underpinnings of business, namely, people and culture. To balance the scales we need to look at how technology must be tempered with a dose of humanity.

In his best-seller, *The Quest for Cosmic Justice,* Thomas Sowell introduces a principle that we think provides great context for cultural issues, trust, and the softer side of the X-economy.[2] Sowell believes that the complexity of modern life has lead us to pursue a misguided

---

[2] Thomas Sowell, *The Quest for Cosmic Justice* (New York: Free Press, 1999).

ideology of righting everything wrong with our world by imposing a set of cosmic values.

According to Sowell, under social values, all things are fair and equal, and change is based on merit—in effect this is the premise for a free market where competition should bring the best products and services to the market. Under cosmic values, all things are *not* fair and equal; therefore, we undertake human intervention as a necessary means to make the world fairer. Sowell's insight is that although the intent behind intervention is understandable, its consequences are often disastrous.

The application of Sowell's argument to social issues, such as equality and justice, is easy to appreciate. But it applies equally to economic institutions.

In many ways, intervention has become the essential value proposition of economics, new economy or old economy. Whether it is the Federal Reserve Bank of the United States adjusting lending rates or global tariffs to promote or dissuade international trade, intervention has become a tool by which we attempt to manage the inherent uncertainty of complex economic system.

With the advent of online exchanges, the same attitudes are now being applied to business. While business has always been, and continues to be, about the search for more efficient exchanges of goods and services, the way that businesses form and manage partnerships and alliances to perform this exchange is changing dramatically—introducing enormous amounts of uncertainty into value chains.

This uncertainty is causing many to look at exchanges as a mechanism of intervention for better controlling commerce. We would propose that exchanges, which are designed, at their very essence, as such an intervention are doomed to fail.

The classic example is that of program trading in stock market exchanges, a form of intervention that was meant to hedge against the inherent risk of market volatilty. The folly of this sort of contrived mechanism to control the market resulted in a massive downward spiral on October 19, 1987.

Unfortunately, it has become vogue to regard resistance to technological mediation or intervention as a Luddite response by an older generation stuck in the past, but there is more at play here than this naïve characterization. If we fluff off these concerns by discounting them and their constituents we are ignoring what is the most basic element of commerce—community.

Community is based on human relationships, for better and for worse. Exchanges must somehow amplify these human relationships, thereby increasing what Sowell calls the social justice of a free market, rather than attempting to create absolute fairness—cosmic justice.

> Process and procedure within an exchange will never (should never) fully replace the judgment of its human participants.

Traditionally, once businesses formed a relationship the partnership was treated with a kind of reverence. In large part that was a means of ensuring stability. Purchasing organizations granted favored status to certain suppliers who formed long-term members of their communities of trade. Today's business models and enabling technologies have altered this age-old static model. Companies now can create and recreate their business relationships based on mutual convenience for short-term gain, lasting only as long as the business need continues, and changing as rapidly as business conditions and circumstances change. As we have already described, trust now takes on a new dimension. Not only are we dealing with the issue of trust between two business partners but the cascading effect of trust amongst an intricate network of organizations and individuals. This is not something that can be solved through technology alone. Process and procedure within an exchange will never (should never) fully replace the judgment of its human participants.

In the X-economy, relationships are at risk of being viewed as commodities, rather than dependable alliances. As easily and quickly as they are formed, they can be dissolved again. Without the traditional steadfast loyalty supporting business partnerships, brands can lose their value and meaning and the critical elements of competitive advantage between one supplier and another may be reduced simply to cost and time; at least in theory.

While it is theoretically possible to create business processes in such a way that they can be moved and shifted and morphed on a whim, the reality is that none of us operates in a perfect world—and probably do not want to. Each business day is full of variable conditions and situations, and the respondents to those conditions are human beings, known to be grossly imperfect resources.

While our business processes and infrastructures have evolved to the point where infinite flexibility is possible, the ability in most organizations to manage and adapt the human resources in a continually changing environment has not kept pace.

Jim Champy, author of the hallmark book on process change *Reengineering the Corporation*[3] states that, companies these days are experiencing difficult times for the following two key reasons:

1. The capacity and capabilities of technology have exceeded our capability to manage and,
2. What we know and what we practice as business strategy doesn't work anymore. Our management processes are behind where they need to be.

As Jim explains it, technology has made a huge amount of information accessible to companies and the individuals within them, but most corporations have yet to learn how to manage this information within their own four walls. The Internet now offers these companies the ability to operate externally, including all the members of the supply chain. The result is a condition, not even so much that of infoglut—which is certainly a huge consideration for companies today—but of not even knowing what it is they don't know. To quote Jim, "The world's an open book, but managers don't know how to access it."

Management is now presented with choices that, on the surface, appear to be technology choices, initially, but whose impact is much

---

[3] Michael Hammer and Jim Champy, *Reengineering the Corporation* (New York: Harper-Business, 1994).

larger. Traditionally, companies seeking to improve business functioning through implementation of new systems were able to work in a three-part, sequential fashion that had them first analyzing their business functions, then identifying and documenting the underlying processes involved, and finally, making a technology choice that fit. In today's world, however, managers no longer have the luxury of sequential, asynchronous activities; technology and business functions are so intertwined, we now cannot consider one without the other. This interdependence forces businesses to make simultaneous, parallel choices that involve the business models and the technology environment that supports them.

The Next Level

Since the shift to an X-economy will mean change throughout an organization—not just technological change, but cultural change—managers must first consider how the organization will overcome the significant cultural obstacles it is bound to face.

> Today's focus is all about breaking out of the ERP-CRM-WWW molds and leaping to the next level: connecting information, employees, customers, and business together in ways that are unimagined today.

For companies that have come into existence only in the last few years, the "e" way is part of the intrinsic culture—they know no other way of doing business. For other companies that have existed for many years, the transformation from "bricks to clicks" is not going to be a simple one. Executives at these organizations will spend the better part of their time managing the transition to the X-economy.

Until now increases in productivity have been all about automating existing business processes. We have been improving those things that we already knew how to do; evolving our processes and procedures and using new technologies to aid us in that evolution.

The X-economy is no longer about incremental evolution. The new frontier is not about automating what already is, but rather the creation of new business activities, abilities, and relationships. As wondrous as we thought them to be at the time, previous paradigm shifts were merely baby steps. Businesses were replacing manual ledgers with spreadsheets. Today's focus is all about breaking out of the ERP-CRM-WWW molds and leaping to the next level: connecting information, employees, customers, and business together in ways that are incomprehensible today.

This transition is far from automatic. Highly functionalized work structures that are deeply embedded in today's corporations are an impediment to flexibility and change. Formerly, the role of technology was primarily that of an enabler of process change. Now the role of technology has expanded, from process enabler to creating new channels to market and enabling new business models.

For many organizations, this metamorphosis is profound. An example of an exchange company that was able to successfully transform a long-standing "bricks" business to a "clicks" world is DoveBid. Prior to their exchange endeavor, DoveBid had 63 years of experience as the world's leading auctioneer and appraiser of capital assets. In 1999, recognizing the ability to use the Internet to accelerate the growth and reach of their business, they began their metamorphosis from their traditional model to a new, on-line presence. In the process, they experienced a number of significant simultaneous changes including: changing from a company that did business in much the same way for over 60 years, to a company using Internet technology and processes; growing from a West Coast-based, largely regional exposure to a global enterprise; evolving from a family-owned business to one that is poised to go public, with all the changes in process, perspective and operations that such a change implies. And, as if all the operational adjustments weren't enough, all these changes took place in only 18 months!

As a result of all these major shifts, DoveBid experienced several challenges during the transformation period. The push toward an exchange model meant that DoveBid would now need to bring in technology-savvy individuals who could implement the new Web-based auction and appraisal application. The entire business culture underwent major changes as the company sought to blend the existing workers who had significant experience and skills in the "traditional" business of asset management with the new technologists. Even the management team at the highest level changed focus as the company modified the mix to now include key members with Internet business experience. The differing perspectives between the old and the new viewpoints affected nearly every decision in the business, from how new employees were hired and what compensation model to use when bringing in people exposed to the high-tech way of doing business, to how capital was raised and growth managed.

However, in spite of all these challenges, DoveBid has been quite successful at this enormous shift in business model and operation. The company has expanded dramatically as a result of the broadened geographical reach and strategic acquisitions that it has made in conjunction with the exchange move in order to supplement its service capabilities and asset categories. Although it has undergone turbulent times during the transformation, DoveBid never considered following any other route to achieve its goals; the asset valuation skills and experience—its true value proposition—were hugely critical and too intrinsic to its core business so that separating the traditional business from the e-business would not have provided a viable solution to its customers.

DoveBid is, however, the exception to the rule. Which is why, for most companies, simply starting over is the best way to move an existing business into the X-economy. The new endeavor, often termed "NewCo" in the business vernacular of the day, can be a spin off from, a subsidiary of the existing company, or it can have an entirely new identity. John Baumstark, an executive vice president at exchange platform player Ariba adds that "the NewCo has the advantage over a transformed existing bricks business of being perceived as neutral in the marketplace." As an example, recall the formation of Covisint in the automobile industry, which we discussed in Chapter 3.

However, starting over isn't without its own set of challenges. When companies spin off a portion of the organization in order to launch an exchange, there can be lasting effects on the existing business as a result of the reorganization around the NewCo. For example, frequently the brightest and the best people in the organization are drafted to join the new endeavor. Subsequently, these people are taken out of their current roles because they are being used to build the new structures. This leaves their coworkers feeling "left behind," and at the same time puts them at a disadvantage, since they now must continue the old work without those colleagues and the knowledge they took with them. Also, smooth continuation of the traditional channel functions are put at risk, since the brightest individuals have already been reappropriated into the exchange.

Ultimately, companies will be forced to change in order to survive. The reasons for moving to an X-economy model are shifting from the desire to gain competitive advantage to a mandate for just keeping up. But, the factors that determine which companies will emerge winners in this transformation are clearly not limited to technology and business models alone.

While there is no silver bullet that will magically eliminate all the potential pitfalls of blending technology innovations with people, there are some fundamental issues that exchanges must consider. And the first of these is that of personalization, which is the subject of the next chapter.

Takeaways

This chapter examined the value of trust as it relates to exchange business models. New technologies have enabled an increase in the pace at which businesses can form and reform value chains in order to create new products and services and, as a result of this there is an increasing volatility in partnerships and alliances. There is less time available to form trust-based relationships. Ultimately, this is what is the limiting factor in the current growth of the X-economy—the very real and often underrated element of trust. Creating marketplaces that engender trust involves overcoming many separate problems in the formation of both the transactions and the relationships. If relationships formed in this new economy are by their very nature becoming more transient, then trust becomes a rare commodity in business partnerships.

The attempts to meet the customers' needs and provide customized, one-to-one solutions to those needs have led us from mass production to mass customization to mass collaboration. The next frontier is peer-to-peer (P2P) communications, in which computers are allowed to talk to each other and share files directly without having to go through an intermediary. While, on the surface, this appears to be in direct contradiction to the exchange model, the type of P2P model as presented in the Napster example, has the site itself providing a function similar to that of the intermediary as represented by the traditional exchange.

In other cases, the exchanges are actually providing sophisticated mechanisms as part of their business model, including services through third-party trust brokers, to help develop confidence and trust on the part of their participants.

The evolution toward a trust-based e-business model across the Web has taken some time to progress through the many opportunistic ways to generate value from the dot.com businesses now in place. But, from the discussions of the X-economy business models and technologies that make it easy for customers to change, it becomes clear that relationships with customers are becoming even more important to the longevity of the business, and a trust-based relationship is a critical factor in maintaining long-term customer loyalty and a means to sustain competitive advantage.

Finally, we looked at some suggestions for dealing with the cultural issues that uncertainty and complexity are sure to create.

CHAPTER 5

Rule 4:
The X-Economy
Is Personalized

*. . . the task is not so much to see what no one yet has seen,
but to think what nobody yet has thought about that which
everybody sees.*

Arthur Schopenhauer

The most profound effect of the Internet has been the
thrashing that results from our inability to manage the
multitude of information sources and resources to
which we suddenly have access.

Along with the all too familiar glut of information we
need to manage and sift through, each of us is constantly jug-
gling a multiplicity of priorities and tasks. The result is a constant bouncing about from project to project, application to
application, information source to information source. This
is precisely the phenomenon we described at the beginning of
the book by using the illustration of the decreasing time we
spend on each individual communication.

The result has been the advent of what might be termed a global attention deficit disorder. It could well be claimed that attention has now become the single most valuable and contested asset of the X-economy.

In his book *The Age of the Spiritual Machine,*[1] Ray Kurtzweil describes how this level of frenetic activity is changing the very nature of time. Significant events in our lives are paced so closely together that they are becoming indistinguishable from one another. It used to be that societal, political, and technological shifts of a transformational nature occurred several times in one's lifetime. We have seen that time frame collapse from a lifetime to a decade to the now popular Internet year.

Psychologists have long known that as the noise factor around us increases, our filtering mechanisms also increase—this is a basic survival skill. It is what scientists refer to as signal to noise ratios. It is the same principle that SETI uses to sniff out intelligent life by scanning the chaotic radio noise of the cosmos for a discernable pattern of intelligence. As the background noise of our world increases, we need to become better at identifying relatively weaker and weaker signals. Yet filtering without accompanying focus can be a dangerous proposition—the equivalent of blinders on a raging plow horse.

Compounding this volume and velocity of information are increasingly shorter windows in which to make decisions. We are weaving the web of our lives ever tighter by dedicating smaller and smaller intervals of attention to each task and responsibility. It's what we call the X-effect—*the volume of opportunity increases and the time to act on each individual opportunity decreases proportionately.* This phenomenon is something you are likely experiencing firsthand. Today, it seems we all have more to do and less time to do it.

For us as individuals this new way of work has not been a gradual change but a sudden shock. It wasn't that long ago when we associated distinct places and times for working, family life, and personal leisure. An eight-hour workday Monday through Friday was the norm;

---

[1] Ray Kurtzweil, *The Age of the Spiritual Machine* (New York: Viking Press, 1999).

evenings and weekends were off limits for work; time for family and home life; leisure fell somewhere in between.

The last decade of the twentieth century saw the most pronounced change in this area. With the advent of the Internet, cellular communications, e-mail, personal satellite communications, wireless network access, and the portability of personal data appliances in a very short period of time, we were suddenly and unpreparedly thrust into a constantly connected mode. Most of us walk through life tagged like wildlife with our pagers, PDAs, and cell phones latched to our belts— not just connected but tethered. The lines of demarcation between the compartments of our lives have become increasingly more vague. Technology links us to work anytime, anywhere. Productivity increases, yet at a high price.

> Yet filtering without accompanying focus can be a dangerous proposition—the equivalent of blinders on a raging plow horse.

From an organizational standpoint, the same principle seems to apply. Value chains are becoming far more intertwined, creating a level of complexity that makes discerning critical events and actions nearly impossible. It's as though we just built a superhighway and then put traffic lights at every on/off ramp.

So what can be done? How do X-economy companies and workers maintain their sanity?

The answer is that companies will need to invest heavily in tools that ease the burden of connectivity by helping employees, customers, and partners control, manage and personalize their interactions, in the face of ever-increasing and portable access.

Portals, single points of personalized access to myriad online resources, are a key factor in attention management; the exercise of capturing mind share against the ever-increasing din of background noise in every marketplace. With a personalized portal, you can create a place, online, where all of the information, people, processes, and applications you need to do your job, make a decision, and collaborate with others is instantly available. If all of this sounds a bit too Orwellian for your taste, consider how basic technologies like the fax machine, cellular phones, pagers, and e-mail have already altered the rhythm of your life.

> Value chains are becoming far more intertwined, creating a level of complexity that makes discerning critical events and actions nearly impossible. It's as though we just built a super-highway and then put traffic lights at every on/off ramp.

The question is not how to break away, but rather how to better integrate and manage the accessibility and complexity that technology provides. X-economy companies take care to acknowledge this and create environments that provide tools for personalizing every experience of their workers, customers and partners. This paves the way for what has quickly become a new generation of "my"-based experiences. It's hardly a surprise, then, that one of the most popular prefixes for Web sites has become the word "My."

If the trend is not yet obvious to you then you need look no further than the amazing differences in how we already work. While the over-40 crowd tends toward work environments that provide focus, those under 30 thrive in work environments that involve a multiplicity of simultaneous tasks and activities.

In either case, there is a need for a highly personalized experience which will bind together the many sources of information and connections that we have to manage. It is this element of personalization that is most essential to managing this increasing burden of complexity and access. And personalization is the principle concept behind the advent of exchange portals.

Toward an X-Economy Desktop

Advances in user interfaces coupled with the enormous decrease in the cost of computing have empowered end users with a wealth of information and computing power at their fingertips. For the enterprise, this means managing widely distributed and heterogeneous information systems that must not only continue to provide individual value, but somehow preserve the value of the entire information base across user communities, in spite of enormous diversity. To fully understand the role and the vision for corporate portals, we need to look closely at the evolution of the working desktop.

At the beginning of the application software era, during the 1970s, we didn't have to worry much about the diversity of platforms, infrastructure, clients, and servers. None of that existed. Information systems architectures were simple; programs were crafted to run directly on the operating environment of the host system.

The constraints of crafting custom programs for each automation need, however, became obvious, and on top of the operating system, we built applications packages to support business systems. Initially these were simple, straightforward applications, to do things like performing basic accounting functions.

But then, the evolution of the desktop continued with the development of host-based models and a common set of applications services and networks to support growth in both the range and the complexity of the kinds of automation that could be delivered. This, however, created a new form of isolation as extensive application customization became the norm. Users quickly realized that applications had to be best-of-breed. The marketing application had to suit the marketing department. The engineering application had to suit the engineering department. And from well-intentioned individuals, acquiring the best tools to do their individual jobs, horribly diverse, fragmented environments developed. This fueled a historic rise in the number of silos, or smokestacks, of highly compartmentalized, segregated information. As the number of these silos and smokestacks increased in functionality and range, they were made ever taller.

As client/server computing began to evolve, individual collections of applications were bundled into process-specific solutions, which aligned with smaller parts of an organization from departments to work groups. Fragmentation became even more pervasive as the number of legacy operating systems and new client/server alternatives made almost all organizations a potpourri of platforms.

This led to the need for technologies that would allow a single metaphor for the use of multiple applications, basic data sharing facilities, and control panel conventions across differing information systems.

In an attempt to unify this increasingly fragmented environment, a desktop technology innovation created the first stop-gap measure: the graphical user interface (GUI) arriving with the Macintosh, X-Windows, and MS Windows. But these environments were, in retrospect, a patch. Their development was an appropriate response to the state of affairs at the time, and it was a step in the right direction. But it was not unification. Does having 20 windows open on your desktop allow you to work more effectively with the information? It clearly does not function to create obvious bonds (links) between the processes that underlie the information and the users' context of need. As long as that information is fragmented at its core, the windows simply reflect, and in some cases magnify, that fragmentation.

We do not underestimate the contribution of "messy desk" windowing systems in the development of our computing environment. Many in the industry rightly credit Xerox/Macintosh windowing technology for contributing a major advance in the mid-1980s by allowing users to cut and paste text and data between applications for the first time. (In fact, the early Macintosh windowing advance—copied and popularized in Microsoft Windows—actually obscured the more fundamental advance in the early Macintosh: the hypermedia development environment HyperCard, which opened the promise of information integration that is currently being fulfilled on the Web.) The core issue is: Can someone looking over your shoulder appreciate what process you are involved in by glancing at your desktop? Is the desktop reflective—in other words, is it obvious when you look at your desktop what process you are involved in? Unlikely.

The work process still resides principally in people's minds; it's not embedded in the corporate memory. That means that there is still no meta-memory that serves as a repository to bridge the discontinuity of a workforce in constant movement. The knowledge of how to do things still depends on specific people or departments. The unconnected windows of the desktop reflect an information-centric view of the world. It is not a business process- or function-centric view of the world, the goal of any exchange that hopes to build value chains from a variety of businesses and competencies.

The advent of the Internet and the widespread deployment of Internet standard technology is now changing the information environment in which this fragmentation has been the unavoidable ruling condition. By providing a new common interface metaphor (the ubiquitous browser) and the basis for an integrated knowledge architecture (or the business operating system we discussed earlier), it is creating the conditions for the arrival of a truly function-centered desktop to replace the application-centered desktop with which we struggle today.

It is not outrageous to predict that within a decade, at most, all talk of applications will fade away. Word processing, spreadsheets, and databases will all become part of a single integrated business environment, in which corporate portals will play a central role in the navigation and delivery of personalized information tools and content. The role of proprietary systems like Microsoft's Windows will be seen as a relic of a former, highly restrictive, and, from a user's viewpoint, unacceptably unproductive era. Windows is the last technology from the age of information scarcity—it was never designed to accommodate the age of information abundance.

We see the emergence of the corporate portal as an initial step in providing a working platform for the age of information abundance, where exchanges will flourish.

Most of us walk through life tagged like wildlife with our pagers, PDAs, and cell phones latched to our belts—not just connected but tethered.

The word *portal* has certainly become the term du jour in circles from Silicon Valley to Wall Street and beyond. Virtually everyone now using Internet technologies inside or outside of the corporate firewall integrates portal visits long or short into their online experience—but why has the concept of a portal become so fascinating to those charged with charting the X-economy? A look at the warp-speed developments on the public Internet portals offers a set of clues.

At the beginning, what we now call portals were referred to as *search engines*. The initial value proposition was bone simple: No one could hope to find anything in the vastness of the Web through "conventional" means so offering a full text index of Web site content provided a great leap forward and a chance to take advantage of the new hyperlinking capabilities built into the Web protocols.

In the next phase of their development, navigation sites became the term used to describe the functions available at Excite, Infoseek, Lycos, and Yahoo. While in the first period, it was assumed that search engine users could navigate around through raw associative webs or links, it soon became evident that developing professional researchers' skill levels in order to find weather information was not high on average users' priority lists. So to address user frustration and reduce the average "seek time" to relevant information, the navigation sites added the function of categorization—filtering popular sites and documents into preconfigured groups by the meaning of their content (sports, news, finance, etc.).

The label then changed once again to *portals*. As portals, the sites not only provide search functionality and a library of categorized content, but they also offered access to communities of interest (e.g., Yahoo! Financial's threaded discussions), real-time chat options, personalization of content by user-specification (my-Excite!), and direct access to specialized functions (shopping networks, auctions, online trading sites, etc.).

At the root of all this change is the constantly articulated proposition that a person should have a single point of access from which to make connections for all their information needs: news, shopping, serendipitous browsing. In fact, that is hardly different from the need businesses have to use online exchanges as a single point of commerce with all of the services and providers necessary to consummate a transaction.

The number of products and applications covered by the market for portals is diverse. Adding to the confusion is the fact that the concept of a portal can be used to describe almost any sort of desktop with network access. To simplify it helps to think of portals as consisting of two basic components, diversity of content and community. Using these dimensions, a simple matrix (see Figure 5.1) can be constructed that classifies any portal application into four categories:

1. *Broadcast portals* are intended for large and diverse communities with diverse interests. These portals tend to follow a fairly traditional broadcasting metaphor, which involves relatively little customization of content except for online search and some interactive capabilities, which would be typical for the Web.

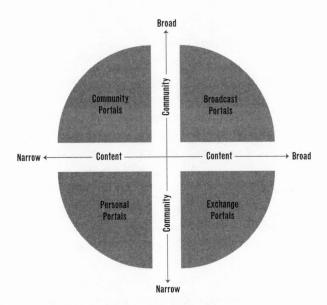

Figure 5.1   Topology of the Portal Landscape. Exchange portals tend to provide a relatively narrow community, such as a set of business partners focusing on the delivery of a specific product or service, with broad content needed to share process and product knowledge and to serve the market.

Popular examples include wsj.com, the interactive version of *The Wall Street Journal* and CNNfn.com.

2. *Community portals* offer narrow content for diverse communities. These are the most popular portals today for online communities. Although they offer customization of the user interface they are still intended for broad audiences and offer fairly simple content (a stock ticker, news on a few preselected items). Community portals are often referred to as channels since they tend to aggregate Web information into a single visual presentation. The most visible of these examples are MyNetscape, MyExcite, and MyYahoo!

3. *Personal portals* target specific filtered information for individuals. Some of these portals, such as Individual Inc.'s fax broadcast, actually predate the Web. As with community portals, they offer relatively narrow content but are typically much more personalized with an effective audience of one. Some of the best examples are found among brokerage houses and online financial sites that provide custom stock portfolios combined with targeted news and analysis.

4. *Exchange portals* coordinate rich content within a relatively narrow community. Since they support decisions core to a particular mission, the term most often used in describing them is *corcasting*. Their portal content is much broader than that of a community portal since there is far greater complexity to the diversity of information used to make decisions in an organization or value chain, as contrasted with the individual deciding to buy or sell stock while reading a press release, a news story, and watching the stocks trading volume. A good example would be to contrast a community portal such as Excite with a Bloomberg terminal in use by a professional stock broker. Although the supported transactions are similar, the latter is clearly an exchange portal.

Exchange portals are increasingly becoming an essential component of an exchange and often end up as the window into the exchange for buyers and sellers. By personalizing what is inherently a very complex transaction an exchange portal can provide a great deal of comfort and familiarity for exchange users. The more complex the transaction and the value chain, the more critical this becomes.

But, the question is "how will this transformation to an exchange portal take place from the many discrete points of interaction in today's value chain?" To answer that question we first need to look at the principle challenges that exchange portals help the businesses to make up a value chain overcome.

Enter the Portals

At the heart of the trend toward personalization is the advent of Internet portals as the dominant means of interacting on the Web. Fueling much of the current confusion about the meaning of the term *portal* is the fact that the concept of a portal can be used to describe almost any sort of desktop with network access. Yet understanding the role of a portal in creating a personalized view of the computer desktop is critical in building businesses for the X-economy.

Portals provide a personalized workspace that integrates our most relevant sources of information and the underlying connections that make this information valuable to us in a single point of access. Portals also learn about our work habits, preferences, and roles in order to provide a constantly changing and personalized experience of the world. The result is a business that is always sensitized to its workers, customers, and partners. Imagine computer-based systems that *know* you.

Portals are intended to address three fundamental challenges that face every X-economy company:

1. Overabundance
2. Discontinuity
3. Information disorganization

Overabundance

The development of the information industry can be read as a continuing story of new opportunities for successful species adaptation created by attractive but unfilled ecological niches arising from the advance of technology. The corporate portal phenomenon is a typical example of creative innovation in the process of this evolution.

The niche for portals has been prepared by the increasing flood of network-accessible electronic information and documents, which has been steadily growing over the past 30 years both from the spread of computer-based business processes in the organization and from the exponential expansion of Internet communications. Over the past few years, the flood has brought about a fundamental shift in the value proposition for information. We have reached a moment in time when the economics of information availability are shifting 180 degrees at the same time the cultural climate supporting communication inside organizations is crumbling (see Discontinuity below).

> The contribution of exchange portals is not simply to help individuals make sense of the volume of information at hand, but more importantly, to help cope with breakdown in our ability to maintain the underlying connections between these information sources—the basis of knowledge.

In all past eras, the overriding negative factor in working with information had been its scarcity—there was never enough available, and decisions had to be made with the certainty that some key missing facts—perhaps the pivotal facts in the decision—would remain unknown to the decision makers. Managers got used to working in this imperfect information environment, and there was never a question about whether the decision makers themselves had the capacity to process whatever information came to hand. Today this situation has been turned on its head. With the nearly universal adoption of corporate intranets, the availability of easy-to-use intranet publishing tools, and, widespread access to the public Internet and its millions of fresh pages daily, scarcity is no longer the issue: overabundance is now the norm. The problem now is the human capacity to process the new quantities of information available.

Examples here abound. In our own experience, we worked with one of the largest U.S. nonprofits in which the higher we looked in the organization's ranks, the greater the amount of time reported just searching for information. The range was from about 10 percent for administrative staff all the way up to 40 percent to 50 percent for senior staff. The weighted average across the entire organization was 18.7 percent, or about one day each week (yes, there are organizations that only work five-day weeks!).

The costs alone are staggering. At one of the world's leading aerospace companies, the average was slightly higher. They actually calculated the cost to the organization on an annual basis as being about $145M/year, and management agreed that this number "sounded" reasonable. (Although, you might wonder if reasonable is simply a relative metric.)

In today's corporate information environment we are experiencing a radical transformation of the relationship between people and the information they have to work with. The incredible influx of readily accessible, yet completely disconnected, sources and streams of information (from Intranets, enterprise applications, electronic business, and the Internet) has made it clear that the means for navigating, organizing, and linking information with underlying business processes is woefully inadequate in most organizations.

Take as an example the situation at Boeing, which is more typical than extraordinary among large organizations today. At one point, Boeing's intranet hosted over 1,600 separate web sites in use by 160,000 users. The rise of interest in corporate portals is a direct response to the need to address this vast but fundamentally chaotic confusion of information.

Most organizations today are unable even to launch a simple full text search across their own intranet, let alone across the full range of information sources across the many partners in a value chain. In fact, our own research has shown that two-thirds of users report lacking this fundamental info-glut management tool.

The contribution of exchange portals is not simply to help individuals make sense of the volume of information at hand, but more importantly, to help cope with breakdown in our ability to maintain the underlying connections between these information sources—the basis of knowledge. When we consider the impact of these issues across multiple business partners throughout a value chain, the effect is to undermine an exchange effort.

Discontinuity

Business reengineering, downsizing, free agency, industry consolidation, merger and acquisition, divestiture, focus on core competencies, global competition, 24/7 operations, jobsharing, telecommuting, the road warrior: all of these trends and dynamics have shaped today's business environment to create the condition of discontinuity for knowledge workers.

Discontinuity's impact is played out not only in a continuously changing set of business conditions outside the office, but more importantly, for the conditions of day-to-day work, it is destabilizing the way work is done inside the workplace. On both an interpersonal and an information systems level, accelerating change is making it difficult for effective work processes to be created or maintained.

The shift to crossfunctional teams and a project approach to many business initiatives has created a work milieu in which peer relationships are fleeting, and job descriptions are temporary at best. As product lifecycles shorten, organizations find themselves in a virtually continual pattern of reorganization: abandoning failing product lines, and regrouping to address new business opportunities.

Portals, as they evolve from pure publishing kiosks to function-centered desktops will begin to provide an antidote to discontinuity (for both knowledge workers and the organization) by capturing the basic patterns of work in the form of a permanent personalized desktop. This goes well beyond simply customizing the graphical presentation, to capturing the relevance and process knowledge inherent in the way an individual works with applications and information. Through this personalized, portal-resident desktop, the discontinuity that results from the movement of workers in a free agent model can be significantly reduced. While not a panacea, the aggregation of information sources in this way provides a mechanism for capturing the connections that make up the value basis for most knowledge worker's environments. In the context of an exchange it provides the ability to create continuity across the many roles and participants of the community.

Information Disorganization

Today, the entire information industry is experiencing a transformation as our view of computer use changes radically from a program-by-program task environment to one that provides information access, delivery, and work support across multiple dimensions of the organization and the value chain.

It is widely understood that applications-based desktops create islands of automation. In spite of the value they have brought to the workplace, they have had the effect of separating and segregating functions and organizations that are intuitively part of the same process.

The situation is analogous to using a different type of phone for every state you want to call. Computer users have suffered this absurdity in quiet indignation from the beginnings of widespread business applications. With the arrival of the possibility of single-access computing, however, it will be no less likely that exchange users will turn on their desktop machine to be greeted by an exchange portal than it is that Internet users today will start up their Web browsers in My Yahoo!

The rapid deployment of intranets over the past two years has alerted application users and IT staff alike to the need for new facilities to identify, capture, store, retrieve, and distribute vast amounts of information from multiple internal and external sources, at an individual, team, or function level.

The result has been that many organizations are pushing the envelope of legacy computing infrastructures and challenging the assumptions of current models of information processing. A movement has begun away from the current state of information systems as a group of isolated "programs" addressing discrete disciplines and toward the engineering of a new ubiquitous information "environment" that will serve as a single, centralized point of information and activity.

This new layer in the business's IT infrastructure is the foundation for corporate portals and the advent of an X-economy desktop.

The Role of the Exchange Portal

Exchange portals offer their participants an environment that is custom-tailored to their needs, which may vary according to differing roles the participant might assume (i.e., buyer, seller, partner, etc.). Similarly, those portals provide their users a highly personalized environment that can be tailored to fit specific needs in order to maximize information access and personalize commerce activities and interactions with the organization's supply chain, facilitating active linkages throughout the integrated community. While portals today differ in the features they offer, we see even the early exchange portal applications providing three key benefits:

1. With an exchange portal, organizations are able to create structured access to information across large, multiple, and disparate value chains.
2. An exchange portal offers a highly personalized view of the exchange for each user.
3. An exchange portal bridges the discontinuity of today's fast companies.

A number of core features allow the portal to take on such an ambitious role:

- The ability to provide automated identification and distribution of relevant content.
- The ability to go beyond search and retrieval to provide content sensitivity.
- The ability to interact intelligently with each user and his or her information activities while providing profiling, filtering, and categorization support to manage information overload.
- The ability to expose the actual, distributed, multienterprise information taxonomy—a task impossible to accomplish through centralized legislation—in other words, no one person knows all aspects of everything they need to know in order to prescribe

how all of the information across a value chain participants should be categorized (also called an information taxonomy).

Unlike today's applications, which deliver automation for discrete elements of work, exchange portals define a new level of information aggregation that radically changes the ability to integrate information, processes, and people across a value chain.

Portal Trends

The portal as defined today can be viewed as either the final application of the data processing era of computing or the very first tool to address the requirements of the new knowledge era. In its current incarnation as information kiosk, it is clearly a retrospective example of a large publishing database. But as interactive applications, from collaboration platforms to vertically focused professional desktops, begin to emerge, the portal will become the platform for tomorrow's function-centered computing.

> The portal as defined today can be viewed as either the final application of the data processing era of computing or the very first tool to address the requirements of the new knowledge era.

At this stage, we can only speculate as to what the resulting landscape of the information industry will resemble in 10 years, once portals have become a standard part of exchanges. What we know for sure is that we will no longer refer to portals, since the range of functionality available from information appliances in many different form factors will have long since left the image of gateway behind.

Each organization will clearly have moved its business model fully into electronic mode, and the last remaining pieces of legacy software from the era of applications will be phasing out. Knowledge workers will have left behind the complaints that the isolation of applications and the contradiction between computer use and productivity made the workplace more frustrating than effective.

In addition to facilitating key processes and information dissemination, exchange portals will improve channel partner effectiveness by focusing not just on how, but *what* information they are receiving. By enabling an outside-in approach to partner communication, the portal establishes a feedback-loop between the manufacturer and its customers and distributors to learn what tools and information will enable the channel partners to most effectively sell their products.

The corporate portal will be regarded as a utility; we will use it to do our work without giving its existence a second thought. Just as we rely on the presence of a dial tone every time we pick up a telephone, we will expect that our personalized work environment will always be available.

It is also clear that we will see the bolstering of business process support in the corporate portal. Workflow, which was once regarded as a stand-alone technology, is now being viewed as an important component of portal architecture; it ties processes together across business partners.

Intelligent agents embedded into vortals working with a preprogrammed or learned set of rules and user preferences will decide whether or not to send a piece of work to a particular business partner. If the appropriate individual or organization is not available to act upon a particular process step that is subject to a time constraint, the agent will route the work to another qualified community member. In addition, these agents will pull information necessary to complete the task from repositories without manual intervention.

Users will demand process design tools that allow them to quickly plan the way that they will interact with external constituents. Exchange portal vendors will be required to include graphical process design tools so managers and business analyst can configure processes on the fly. If simple tools, including libraries of customizable vertically oriented processes templates are not provided, users will face the same sort of bottleneck that existed in the early days of intranets, when a

Webmaster was required to translate any document to HTML before it could be made available to users. Companies will not be able to move at e-business speed if managers must wait for an IT staff member to build the electronic processes required to interact with new partners and customers from scratch.

To this end, one of the most effective approaches a manufacturer might take is to adopt an "inside-out" perspective that profiles a day in the life of its various channel and customer participants, then use that perspective to help those participants be more successful in those targeted activities.

Do not be misled, however, by the apparent simplicity of portals. Effectively implementing such an outside-in approach can prove a daunting task, particularly in the face of organizational and cultural resistance. Few large organizations have in place reward structures that incent risk taking along these lines. And, putting these reward structures in place is difficult enough within the organization; how do you motivate and enforce participation with external members? You begin by turning the value chain inside-out.

Turning the Value Chain Inside-Out

For the last half of this century, each new decade has experienced a major redefinition of the buyer/seller relationship. From the Main Street of the 1950s emerged the local shopping centers of the 1960s, evolving to the strip-malls of the 1970s, then the megamalls of the 1980s, and finally the "big box" superstores of the 1990s.

Just as the large chains have largely replaced the corner grocer, the superstores and "category killers" have displaced the five-and-dimes and local appliance dealers that once adorned Main Street USA. Each new decade has resulted in the radical redefinition of business models, often evolving faster than incumbents can react.

This phenomenon is not unique to the consumer retail market but is at the heart (or perhaps more aptly, the throat) of every industry. Fueling this movement are increasingly sophisticated customers, seeking greater choices and availability of products. With each generation, a new modality of commerce has evolved in response to better-educated buyers with heightened expectations.

Driven by both customer demand for a single-point-of-service and resellers' desire to expand sales by offering new product options, the banking, insurance, and financial services industries have evolved from a segmented, buy-direct modality to an integrated business model where the once clear lines of differentiation have been blurred beyond recognition.

Over time, the supporting activities of any single transaction have grown into an increasingly complex network of constituencies. What was once a simple exchange between a buyer and seller is now represented by an elaborate value chain comprised of resellers, wholesalers, component suppliers, distributors, value-added manufacturers, and, ultimately, the end customer. The transparent coordination of this value chain is critical to the commercial viability of any business.

Consider the example of Wal-Mart, widely held as a role model for the most recent commerce paradigm. The secret to Wal-Mart's success is not the exclusivity of the products they offer, but rather their now famous system for managing suppliers and inventory. This has evolved into a Byzantine web of business-to-business interactions and transactions, where substantial investments in technology and rigorous requirements of participant vendors have provided Wal-Mart with the foundation of their competitive advantage.

The trend-line that follows the evolution of business models over the past several decades is defined by exponentially increasing value-chain complexity.

Driven by both customer demand for a single-point-of-service and resellers' desire to expand sales by offering new product options, the banking, insurance, and financial services industries have evolved from a segmented, buy-direct modality to an integrated business model where the once clear lines of differentiation have been blurred beyond recognition. While mergers and acquisitions have fueled some of this, the vast majority of business is the result of a complex, multifaced sales channel.

In the information technology arena similar forces have given rise to large distributors such as Tech Data, as well as thousands of value-added resellers (VARs), who collectively represent the majority of all IT purchases. Increasingly, original equipment manufacturers (OEMs), or the companies who build the products these distributors sell, have come to rely on these channels for the majority if not all of their business.

The idea is familiar if you are one of the majority of businesses on either side of this equation assembling a network of sales agents to leverage sales and marketing across multiple channels in exchange for a percentage of sales revenue. This intermediated model allows the sales organization to scale faster than if it were grown organically and frees the manufacturer to focus on the development process. The indirect channel is able to sell products it would be otherwise unable to develop on its own. As straightforward as it may seem, however, this arrangement comes with a cost to both parties.

The Hidden Cost of Intermediation

The blame for reducing profit margins in this new era of business is often placed at the feet of price-based competition. However, the real culprit is well below the surface.

On top of the discounts in revenue involved with distributing sales proceeds among each contributing party, margins further shrink as a result of the lack of efficiency, and resulting transfer costs associated with the greater levels of complexity in the sales process. With each new participant entered into the equation, the effort involved with co-ordination grew exponentially.

This is a function of not only those costs incurred vis-à-vis the physical movement of goods from one party to another, but also the cost of educating and supporting the downline sales channel. Further inefficiencies persist as a result of disconnects in the feedback loop between the buyer and builder of the product. Each layer that separates the manufacturer from the end-user further dulls their sensitivity to market trends and delays responsiveness.

Another area of significantly increased costs is that of post-sales support of end-users. This burden is no less than that with goods and services sold directly, despite the lower margins associated with indirect sales. Whether the distributor or the manufacturer carries the onus of support, the sting of this burden is always greater when subsidized by only a fraction of sales proceeds.

In response, distributors and resellers have instituted a variety of systems and procedures to rein in these costs and inefficiencies, which are often viewed as Draconian by suppliers since they are significantly skewed in favor of the resellers and require substantial support resources, drastic price discounts, and zero tolerance of defects.

It is not surprising that to date most efforts to increase value-chain efficiency have focused on the supply chain. After all, the distributor holds the greatest leverage—they control the customer relationship so why wouldn't they call the shots for their suppliers? However, the value chain is a two-way street, involving the downstream process, the supply chain, as well as the upstream process, the demand chain.

Suppliers in an intermediated sales process must contend with the challenges of channel management, in many cases supporting both external channels as well as an internal sales force. All communications and documentation must be filtered for each constituency's role and responsibility, dramatically increasing the support burden and often adding bottlenecks to the process of distributing information.

The ultimate goal of managing the demand chain effectively is to enable the downstream partners to more effectively sell the manufacturer's products over those of competitors. This is often in the face of eroding (or completely severed) relationships between manufacturer and end-users, which severely diminishes the level of control over what and how its products are sold, or respond in time to customer trends.

Issues such as the quality of information and customer relationships may on the surface appear to be supply chain issues, but indeed they are matters of the demand chain. The manufacturer is the greatest stakeholder here, and he must bear the fallout of mismanaged up-stream events. The challenge manufacturers face is to keep the indi-rect channel in check in an environment often insensitive to the challenges and problems often felt by the manufacturer alone.

This places the responsibility on the manufacturer to refocus channel partners on supporting their products by directly facilitating this aspect in their day-to-day jobs, providing them with the tools to best communicate with their customers, and overall to being easy to do business with. For many manufacturers, this has meant creating an army of field representatives to support the channel partners. How-ever, this has added a new level of complexity to the sales process and further erodes the shrinking margins of distributed sales model.

The New Challenge of Disintermediation

In response to the problems above and overall shrinking margins, an undercurrent of disintermediation has evolved where manufacturers are seeking to eliminate intermediaries and sell directly. This trend was perhaps most noticeable in consumer sectors, beginning with a prolifer-ation of buy-direct catalogues in the 1980s. In the 1990s, product man-ufacturers from Nike and Sony to thousands of smaller companies have thrown down the gauntlet to superstores and category killers by open-ing their own chains of specialty outlet stores.

This trend has continued down both paths of direct mail and di-rect retail, eventually moving into the realm of business-to-business commerce. The distinction between traditional direct sales and the disintermediated model is that in place of a sales force a specific com-munication piece (e.g., a catalogue) is sent to a broad array of poten-tial customers in the hope of generating inbound sales. Over the past decade, many manufacturers ranging from Apple and IBM to furni-ture makers and financial service companies have explored this model, with varying levels of commitment and equally varied success.

However, the wellspring of disintermediation has come from the worldwide market of millions of potential customers found in the

Web. Manufacturers saw in the Internet's promise of rich, ubiquitous, low cost communication an opportunity to go around their distribution channels and sell directly to their end customers. Inspired by now infamous success stories such as Dell, disintermediation has been the rallying cry of electronic commerce initiatives. For many it is, or was, the obvious answer to many of the problems we've mentioned so far. Why give up that margin if you don't have to? Why spend so much time supporting a field sales staff over whom you have no direct control. Why kowtow to the demands of dealers who remain the immovable block between you and your end-users?

But too many manufacturers have jumped in without a full appreciation of the consequences. Namely, when 80 percent to 90 percent of your revenue comes from an indirect channel, how will they react to you becoming their direct competitor? In many cases, their reaction is to quickly drop you in favor of your competitor, taking your end-users with them.

Consider this familiar scenario: The rep from the dealer where you previously purchased a product calls to tell you that it is no longer supported by them, but that they are happy to upgrade you to its replacement. Was this really due to inadequacy or simply that the product's manufacturer just became their disintermediated competitor? If you are like most users, the question never crossed your mind if your experience with the dealer was favorable (perhaps in no small part due to the support they received from the manufacturer). How would this scenario play against your channel?

For the companies who have not yet embraced the distintermediation opportunity of the Web, the risk of indirect channel revenue is becoming clear vis-à-vis the growing number of examples of those who had jumped in headfirst with their eyes shut. Those fortunate early adopters of direct Web-based strategy able to survive this leap of faith are today scrambling to reestablish their indirect channel. For these companies and the pragmatic holdouts that have resisted the siren song of disintermediation, a new opportunity has emerged to redeploy the same capabilities of the Web in a way that empowers, rather than isolates the indirect sales channel.

This hybrid selling sales model exists together with a manufacturer's direct sales efforts, supporting new distribution relationships with the same capabilities used to improve the performance of direct sales teams and cultivate relationships with direct customers. Rather than removing intermediaries, this new modality reintroduces, or "reintermediates" the sales channel. And this is where the portal plays its most important role.

The next Dell or great Internet economy hero will not come from a disintermediated sales strategy, but rather a company that leverages the ubiquity and accessibility of the Web to link all stakeholders in the sales process. Called *re-intermediation,* this allows manufacturers to create mindshare among customers, prospects, and sales agents by creating new personalized channels for disseminating product and company information out to multiple parties in the proper format and context. For example, promotional information is distributed among prospects, along with links to the appropriate channel contacts based on the prospect's profile. Field sales reps and other channel sales participants receive sales support info, personalized based on their specific roles and relationships. End-users receive, or can directly request, product support information that is tailored to their own industry, installation, or interests.

All of this requires a new level of technology to support the extraordinarily personalized interactions required forming reintermediated value chains. This capability is enabled by a new solution approach that packages the capabilities of the portal and makes this available across the entire value chain.

Portals provide an integrated and personalized operating environment that serves as a centralized point for linking all our information sources and applications in a way that streamlines work processes. Portals have the ability to learn about and adapt to our work habits, preferences, and functions, thereby increasing their personalization capabilities to better suit a constantly changing e-business environment.

Portals also allows this personalized content to be integrated into intra- and inter-organizational process management. The result is increased loyalty among partners and customers.

Takeaways

As technology has allowed us access to more and more information, our ability to adequately process it, even with the multitude of tools and techniques at our disposal have hardly kept pace. In fact, it is this smorgasbord of inputs and applications that have us in a continual flurry of activity, hopping from one project to the next, from one application to another. The increasingly shorter windows we have in which to handle tasks and make decisions causes us to do more and more in less time: *The volume of opportunity increases and the time to act on each individual opportunity decreases proportionately.* This chapter has dealt with the natural result of this condition—a global attention deficit disorder—and the new capabilities being developed to help us cure it.

One way in which X-economy companies are assisting in the solution is by creating environments that offer tools for personalizing the experiences of their workers and community members. Personalization supplies one of the keys to managing the incredible amount of infoglut and processing complexity.

Portals have been developed as an important tool for managing this complexity by providing single-point, personalized access to information and applications. Portals are intended to address three fundamental challenges that face every X-economy company:

1. Overabundance
2. Discontinuity
3. Information disorganization.

Portals can serve as valuable tools not only to the organization's internal workers, but also can be extended to include the entire organization's value chain of suppliers, vendors, and other business partners. But expanding the business to essentially include the value chain as part of an integral whole does not come without its own set of challenges and costs.

While the organization may see a huge benefit to the potential added channel the Web presents, business partners involved in the traditional channel may see technology as a threat and have concerns about being disintermediated by the new model. The key to business longevity will be to understand how to use the X-economy models to link all stakeholders to their mutual benefit. This linkage is the process of reintermediation—bringing these stakeholders back into the value chain.

CHAPTER 6

Rule 5:
The X-Economy
Is Instantaneous,
Get Used to It

Faster! Faster! Until the thrill of speed overcomes the fear of death!

Hunter S. Thompson, *Fear and Loathing in Las Vegas*

There is more to life than increasing its speed.

Mahatma Gandhi

Redefining Time

At 9 P.M. on Christmas Eve in 1906, Reginald Aubrey Fessenden changed the meaning of community forever at Brant Rock Station in Massachusetts. It was there that Fessenden transmitted the first wireless radio transmission consisting of more than mere dots and dashes.

An ocean away a handful of passengers on ships in the middle of the Atlantic were, for the first time in mankind's existence, connected in real time to the intimate sounds of another human being beyond the reach of their voice. Christmas wishes and a few lines of scripture to the tune of "Oh Holy Night," on a violin heralded the era of electronic community.

The metronome of our lives is governed primarily by our ability to make connections. The frequency of connections defines the measure of time, and it makes little difference if we are describing a biological organism, a silicon wafer, an organization, or a marketplace.

In the X-economy, these connections are forcing time-based competition on every element of the supply chain in every industry.

The changes in the information technology industry have been particularly obvious and well-documented. In the semiconductor area, Moore's law (as re-analyzed by Kurzweil in 1998) has meant entirely new processor product lifecycles and falling performance/prices, on a two-year pattern since the 1960s. Even at the other end of the information technology product spectrum, in consumer-targeted desktop printers, for example, lifecycles are shorter than one year and still compressing.

Outside of information technology, in areas like pharmaceuticals and automotive manufacturing, the ability to create entire new market opportunities with products like Viagra or the luxury-class sports utility vehicle is becoming literally a prerequisite for business survival.

The most extreme example of the new realities of time competition, however, is now codified in the Silicon Valley vernacular becoming part of the worldwide language: the concept of Internet time. In this new rationalization, competitive time in the Internet markets is effectively like "dog years," and several cycles can take place in the course of a few calendar months. Companies like Yahoo! and Amazon.com have built brands of impressive strength with financial valuations undreamed of just a few short Internet years ago. Clearly these events are changing one of the basic elements of the business environment in fundamental ways.

The profound economic and competitive realities associated with the arrival of full-blown time competition is still only dawning on most managers today. To appreciate the radical impact of the change on both the economics of competition and the nature of the Internet-time organization, we quote from Stan Davis' seminal description of the new reality:

> To understand this transformed notion of time, let's take an example from the physical world: sound traveling through time. Sound travels at the speed of about 660 miles per hour. Think of two airplanes, one sub-sonic and the other supersonic, traveling from point (1) to (2). The sound emitted from the subsonic plane reaches point (2) at the same time the plane does. The supersonic plane, however, reaches point (2) before its sound does.
>
> Imagine arriving in a place at (2) and then waiting for the arrival of your own sound. In this context, you are there before the fact. You have created a phenomenon, gotten ahead of it after it was created, and observed it catch up with you.
>
> In this example of sound traveling through time, the lag between the two points in time is so brief that there is not much more one can do than observe the occurrence. But if one takes the essence of the act, it is possible to conceive of the lag as an indefinite period of time. During this extended period of being someplace that has not yet happened, the pilot/manager can be very busy preparing for the arrival of the sound. Similarly, the manager can be very busy managing the arrival of the organization that will be appropriate for the time when it arrives.[1]

Although Davis could not have anticipated this in the mid-80s, don't managers at firms like Amazon.com and Yahoo! have exactly the luxury today that he described: continually busying themselves with the arrangements for the future market while their competitors struggle to catch up to where they had been yesterday? Increasingly, survivor companies today will be learning how to achieve the same advantage.

Although the fundamentals of commerce have remained essentially the same throughout the history of economic man, what has changed radically in just the last decade is the notion of lag time. Our ability to form connections faster has provided the firmament for industries to dis-integrate into much broader and more complex value chains.

---

[1] Stanley M. Davis, *Future Perfect* (Boston: Perseus Press, September 1996).

Today, buyers take for granted the ability to find information on goods and services at the click of a mouse; now sellers have to scramble to keep up. This attitudinal shift has filtered through the entire value chain. And it is this shift that, more than anything else, has brought the exchanges to center stage.

The formation of exchanges is in direct response to this, and the resulting overnight disappearance of the latency in market interactions, which, along with every other aspect of our organizations, began to vanish as the pace of life accelerated. With little or no lag time in transactions, both buyers and sellers have become ever more conscious of time as the principle metric of success.

Today, buyers take for granted the ability to find information on goods and services at the click of a mouse; now sellers have to scramble to keep up. This attitudinal shift has filtered through the entire value chain. And it is this shift that, more than anything else, has brought the exchanges to center stage. Since it is no longer the realm of any one business to suit the needs of the consumer but rather a cacophony of interrelated business partners, coordination across each is essential to achieve competitive responsiveness. As innovative velocity and consumer pull accelerate, these networks are unceasingly increasing in complexity.

Building these intricate networks is not trivial. Successful companies have historically been those who created a fortress around their supply and demand chains and who could effectively rebuild them for new innovations.

But in a demand-driven market where customers configure their own products and services, the luxury of response time is eliminated. Exchanges create an asynchronous and nearly instantaneously responsive market.

Exchanges establish the ground rules for being a buyer or a seller in these demand-driven value chains, mediating the countless relationships between buyer and seller. In this nearly frictionless market the exchanges become the defining construct for business in the new millennium.

Building Intimate Markets

One of the most basic and apparent contradictions of the X-economy is the problem that has plagued organizations throughout the industrial era—highly specialized work forces create a *lack* of intimacy. Simply put, increasing specialization in complex organizations tends to isolate workers, customers, and partners from one another, and one's knowledge of what others in the organization actually do is scant, or perhaps even non-existent. Where once the isolation was structural (i.e., built into the organizational structure of the workplace), today it is more likely that space, distance, and time are the factors that work against intimacy.

If dis-integration is an essential feature of the X-economy, one has to ask if we are not going to be exacerbating the problem of lacking intimacy through even further specialization.

Absolutely not.

When two people are separated by several days in performing their respective tasks on a particular value chain of activities, the reality is that they are less likely to understand the impact of one another's work than if they were separated by hours or minutes. Why? In a word, *iteration*. The longer it takes to iterate a task, the less likely it is to be iterated. In other words, if it takes you two days to get a response to a question as opposed to two minutes, you are less likely to ask the question. By the same token, you are less likely to try to understand or change a process if you are removed from its components by significant intervals of time.

X-economy companies close the time intervals by eliminating the inherent transfer times in routing information and work from one person or one organization to another. But it's useful to note that this is not a problem that can be solved by a communications network alone, no more so than it can be solved by the evolution from paper memos to e-mail. Electrons may travel at the speed of light, but work and people do not.

> Organizations have focused for too long on the delivery of information and the delivery of work. Work, by its definition, is not delivered—it is performed.

If you don't believe that, ask yourself this question: When did I last read my e-mail? If it was two hours ago, then you could say that the e-mail messages waiting for you have taken at least that long to get from their sender to you, although the actual message traveled at the speed of light and probably took mere nanoseconds to be delivered. The same is true for work of any sort being delivered electronically. Part of the problem is that organizations have focused for too long on the delivery of *information* and the delivery of *work*. Work, by its definition, is not delivered—it is performed. No matter how fast the assembly line runs, the work will always end up waiting without the right tools to connect it with the performer of the work.

The transformation to intimacy does not happen suddenly to either organizations or their markets. For a business to achieve intimacy it must go beyond the networking of information alone by using sophisticated mechanisms to route work and deliver it in the fastest possible period of time. This may include using *roles* or expert brokering systems to route the work to a particular skill set instead of a specific person. In such a case, if one person, who would normally do the work, is not available to act on the work, the business should find someone else with similar qualifications to perform it. The key is getting the work done—not just transferring the information. This is often referred to as a *pull model*, as opposed to a push model of work.

In the pull model, a manager doesn't have to hunt down the right person to get the work done; instead the manager goes after the role. For instance, in one large software support organization, the system identifies how incoming support calls are routed to individuals based on predefined skill sets. In another case, a major defense contractor's approval routing systems for proposed contract changes is intelligent enough to know that a number of people can fill the role of approver and routes the approval based on availability.

At the simplest level, take any firm that requires a continuous, possibly nonlinear, flow of materials or goods for its proper function and service to its own customers. The company may be directly connected to several suppliers, for the same or differing items. And when there is an order or a discussion for a product to be delivered on a specific date, it can be instantly known and the system makes decisions for order fulfillment by the best-equipped or most available supplier. The intelligence here comes from the setting of parameters, such as supplier capacity and known values such as work-in-progress and scheduled capacities of various suppliers, specific talent of individuals, travel time, available raw materials and inventory control for the ultimate in Just-in-Time system. Observe any number of large manufacturing industries and there are many variations of this currently being used.

The other effect that roles tend to have on an organization is that of increasing the critical analysis of any process. In the same way that a single role can be filled by a number of people, a single person may have multiple roles, since it is entirely likely that a single person can have multiple skills. As a result, work tends to be distributed across a broader range of individuals within the organization, creating less parochialism and thus avoiding the "this is the way it's done" syndrome that makes so many processes stale.

Ironically, the traditional push model works best for employees who perform relatively poorly and worst for those employees who are most productive and responsive. The reason is simply that work tends to congregate around productive people, creating an imbalance. Knowledge is punishment in this model, since the rewards for work well done are an ever-increasing workload. Pull models tend to distribute work more equitably among all workers defined by a particular role. Additionally, the pull model can be used to create more equitable forms of compensation for workers, as we will see in the case studies discussed later in this chapter.

X-economy companies believe strongly in this equity and create environments that recognize it. By doing so they are reaffirming the value of the individual by increasing process involvement, critical analysis, and process intimacy across the organization.

Asynchronous Markets

Your railroad, when you come to understand it, is only a device for making the world smaller.
Ruskin

There are two fundamentally polar means by which humans communicate: synchronous and asynchronous communication.

Standard interpersonal communications occur in a synchronous mode. That is, when two or more people conduct a discussion, they are able to communicate at the same time and possibly (but not necessarily) in the same place. A face-to-face meeting or telephone call is perhaps the most common setting for synchronous communication. A benefit often attributed to synchronous communication is the ability to address issues as they arise without delay.

The explosive growth in global communications technology and software for communication, including the world-wide web, e-mail, and groupware, have allowed companies to take advantage of asynchronous communication; that is, the ability to communicate serially, without interaction and interruption, thereby bridging the constraints of time and distance.

For centuries, the only form of asynchronous communication was that of the written word or image. The cave paintings of Lascaux, Egyptian steles, and the Dead Sea Scrolls, for example, have communicated ideas and thoughts across social and political chasms spanning thousands of years. The most common form of asynchronous communication in modern times has been the letter: One person writes to another and then waits for a reply. Synchronous communication on the other hand has, until very recently in the history of mankind, been limited by the confines of distance; quite literally, by how far could one's voice be heard.

A quantum leap in asynchronous communication came in 1844, with the invention of the telegraph. As a result, the speed of asynchronous communication was vastly increased. Moreover, distance became largely irrelevant; as long as wires could connect Site A to Site B, communication could take place. At first, telegraph lines crisscrossed the United States and were a critical factor in the development of railroads.

When the great railroads first established transcontinental lines, one of the most serious problems to be overcome was that of head-on collisions. At that time it was not very cost-effective to put two lines in services for each route, so a single line handled both directions of traffic. Coordinating this prior to the availability of the telegraph presented a serious problem.[2]

Although the telegraph brought us closer to continental synchronous communication, it was still limited by geography and the basic requirement of a telegraph operator who could translate the electronic gibberish. True synchronous communication was still limited by shouting distance.

By 1869, however, much of this had been resolved. With the first transatlantic telegraph cable, linking North America with Great Britain and the invention of the telephone in 1876, distance became largely irrelevant to synchronous communication.

Since then, telephony has remained the mainstay of business communication, enhanced by such innovations as satellite transmission and fiber optics. Although aided by other common modes of asynchronous communication including e-mail and voice mail, the process of communication has never gained the most important aspect of true synchronous communication, which is its connection with the underlying process being communicated. This linkage is a difficult, but an essential, point in understanding the creation of an X-economy.

What we have just described may seem like an insurmountable problem. After all, X-economy businesses cannot alter the laws of time and physics. But they can eliminate the fundamental obstacles in asynchronous communication, the lack of concurrence of human communication and the difficulty in bringing people together. In the X-economy, asynchronous communication can continue even though the people are not working on a synchronized schedule by using the exchange as the persistent intermediary.

---

[2] Eventually, all trains carried a "telegrapher" who was armed with a "relay box" that could be attached to telegraph wires by the roadbed in order to receive instructions from a dispatcher or call for assistance. Brown, Dee, *Hear That Lonesome Whistle Blow: Railroads and the West* (New York: Touchstone Books, 1977), p. 179.

The first generation of tools to do this is already appearing on the web with sites such as Guru.com, Advoco.com, ExpertNet.com, DejaNews.com and Epinions.com. One of these new expert brokers, Inforocket, combines expert brokering with a reverse market model to bring together people with question and answers. Questions are submitted and experts who have answers can bid on the cost of the advice. The buyer chooses the expert based on their ranking with other buyers of advice, their profile, and their bid.

Other approaches provide expert brokering solutions that can actually scour a business intranet, observe how people interact with their computer desktop, e-mail, word processing documents and develop profiles of expertise automatically.

With a constantly up-to-date library of expertise across an enterprise, value chain, or market, the foundation for instantly bringing together the skills needed for a particular task is in place. However, the problem of bringing the people together in the same time, even if not in the same place, is still a problem. Which is where we see yet another set of tools on the horizon.

These technologies will provide the ability to either track experts or to use agents to act as surrogates for experts. These are akin to having an assistant who knows you, your expertise, and the many nuances of how you prefer to interact with others and is available 24 hours, seven days a week to help others who need you get answers to their questions or get in contact with you. In other words, the process continues despite the unavailability of the people.

Intimacy is not defined necessarily by interactions of person to person but in the nature and depth of the relationships, which are defined by the interconnectivity of the concerned parties. Entities interconnected in an exchange will be intimately involved in one another's scheduling, external functions and other business processes. Knowledge as a result of connectivity will breed intelligence, which can support business intuition and instinct. As each industry model becomes interconnected, they all become increasingly interdependent.

Perhaps the most pronounced manifestation of intimacy is in the emerging domain of e-learning. We see this as being one of the most significant support mechanisms and propellants for the X-economy.

E-Learning

During the entirety of the industrial era, our focus was on moving work to the workers. From supply chain to assembly line, transportation systems to information systems we built enormously complex infrastructures to ensure that work and work products arrived at the right time at the right place. But what of the tools and the knowledge needed to do the work?

As exchanges begin to scale the increasing flow of transactions and the volume of partnerships being formed within an exchange environment will require that we revisit many of the basic assumptions surrounding the issues of training. In short, our ability to learn has to equal the pace of innovation in the value chain.

The principle behind e-learning is that the tools and knowledge needed to perform work, are moved to the workers—wherever and whoever they are. Simply put, e-learning revolves around people—in stark contrast to the way learning has typically involved people flocking around the learning.

This is not a revolutionary concept when applied on a small scale, but when considered in the high-velocity context of the X-economy, it directly challenges what is perhaps the most important advancement of modern society and the cornerstone of academic learning: the growth of the centralized institution of education, in which students came to a specific time and place to learn.

> Simply put, e-learning revolves around the individual—in stark contrast to the way training has typically involved individuals flocking around institutions of learning.

Since the time of Plato's Academy, students have trooped off to schools, universities, all manner of brick, mortar, and ivy-clad buildings of learning. The idea of the university—often an empire unto itself—looms large in the collective consciousness of industrial man.

This was a large part of the industrial ethos that led to the sort of work and worker that was captured perfectly in the 1936 film *Modern Times*. Who can forget the image of the hapless Charlie Chaplin tightening bolts on a large flywheel? Along with his fellow workers, Chaplin had been minted in lots by the educational factories to be yet another cog in the machine.

The modern value chain is still very much like those flywheel cogs, discriminating between people, steps, and procedures. Specialization and highly distributed operations have created monstrously complex interactions between business partners.

E-learning is not merely an alternative means of training, but a profound shift in the manner by which organizations are supporting the complex, volatile, high-velocity value chains of the X-economy. *E-learning is just-in-time education integrated with high-velocity value chains.*

E-learning had its origins in computer-based training (CBT), an attempt to automate education, replace a paid instructor, and develop self-paced learning. But E-learning should not be confused with traditional forms of computer-based training (CBT), which are nothing more than recorded education. It is also a subject that needs to be separated from the legacy of academic learning that has so clearly defined our notions of education.

> E-learning should not be confused with traditional forms of computer-based training (CBT), which are nothing more than recorded education.

In the mid-twentieth century, workers spent the first 20 years of their lives training to work another 40. As technology entered the office and factory floor, individuals found themselves spending a greater amount of their working lives learning such things as how to use PCs, new software applications, business processes and so forth, instead of actually contributing to core business objectives. Yet, as the rate of change and innovation across all industries increases while at the same time the volume of information grows, we have reached a state of grid-lock where most of us spend too much time jumping from subject to subject struggling to keep pace. We have become a society of thrashers, with increasingly smaller intervals of time to dedicate to any one task—the proverbial jacks of all trades, experts of none.

In the jump to the late twentieth century shortening product life-cycles, increasing time-to-market pressures, and a dearth of skilled workers served as a reveille for corporations to wake up and realize that they needed to do more with existing human capital. Use of automation, corporate restructuring, and geographic reassignment only went so far. As these maladies were putting pressure on growth, corporations decided to throw money into information technology infra-structure. But since complexity usually scales with functionality, the return on these investments was elusive.

Today, in the wake of the ERP debacles of the 1990s, organizations have realized just how ill-equipped they are to deal with major changes in technology and processes, and how quickly these technologies and the processes they support change.

The conclusion is obvious: Given that knowledge is our stock in trade, we need to constantly find new ways to synchronize the knowl-edge of workers with their work environment. Having the appropriate intellectual horsepower in place is more important than possessing the latest in bleeding edge technology, processes, and products. We are al-ready seeing that one profound effect of exchanges is the immediate and wholesale destruction of the walls built up over decades between the working parts of the extended enterprise—its customers, its sup-pliers, its partners, its people. The entire scope of relationships in vital value chains is being rethought and realigned by new e-business rela-tionships. And, as that occurs, it is evident that anyone involved in these processes—anyone with a *need to know*—must be trained, edu-cated, or reeducated to effectively perform their work. This, the whole-sale education and training up and down the value chain, is the primary role of e-learning, and a necessary part of a well thought out exchange.

Without e-learning firmly in place, the X-economy will quickly stall as skills fall well behind the potential for new innovations and liquidity.

Bridging Knowledge Asymmetry

It comes as no surprise that intellectual property and human capital have become the most important resources in the twenty-first century. This is a mantra that is now common in the hallways of every organization. Maximizing the utility of these assets and competing in the new economy requires that skills and knowledge become as much a part of the supply chain as office supplies, inventory, and computers: all need to be available instantly at appropriate times and in the proper quantities for each task and worker. This just-in-time aspect of business in the new economy is the essence of e-learning.

> We have to accept that learning is no longer simply a matter of continuous improvement but rather a fundamental part of corporate strategy.

As organizations grow more complicated, it is not just information that becomes more difficult to capture but also the information about the information—that is, the knowledge of what to do with the information and how to use it in support of enterprise processes, partners, and customers. However, as each of these three constituencies moves at ever-increasing velocity, knowledge is lost by miscommunication, time lags, and turnover. The result is an enormous asymmetry in the underlying knowledge needed to support each aspect of the value chain. E-learning prevents, or at least mitigates, these asymmetries and strengthens the glue that holds organizations and value chains together.

The power of e-learning rests its ability to deliver both the richness and reach needed to maximize the effectiveness of the learning process. Richness in presentation is provided by multimedia technologies, allowing both live classroom experiences, as well as asynchronous modes which include audio and video. Content richness is provided by blending off-the-shelf learning materials with custom materials and internal knowledge. E-learning's reach is provided by its flexibility, distance learning capabilities, and collaborative technologies.

An ancient Chinese proverb is, "Give me a fish and I eat today: teach me to fish and I eat for a lifetime." We have to accept that learning is no longer simply a matter of continuous improvement but rather a fundamental part of corporate strategy; our people must all become anglers of, by, and for e-learning. In fact, as competitive pressures escalate, companies will grow less tolerant of the critical skill gap that exists between the abilities of the average workers and peak performers. As the demand for skilled workers naturally increases, this gap will grow larger. E-learning is a crucial weapon in conquering this competitive disadvantage.

It is essential to understand that the differences between training and e-learning are not just semantic. The nine distinct ways in which training of any sort, be it classroom or computer-based, and e-learning differ are shown in Figure 6.1.

Redefining Learning

There will always be a need for training, but its role has shifted to one primarily remedial in nature. Society has, for the most part, accepted the notion of lifelong learning for all. E-learning encompasses both, but adds knowledge management as a value to organizations. The blistering pace with which technologies, business models, products, services, and marketplaces have proliferated over the past decade exceeds our capability to keep up by using traditional corporate training paradigms. Unfortunately, there has been little improvement in the traditional methods used by most organizations to communicate changes and updates to employees, suppliers, partners, and customers. This lack of progress has created a widening rift with the potential to create a severe bottleneck in the growth of any organization, and may well represent the greatest threat to continued global economic expansion.

Low unemployment and a near dearth of available skilled workers have moved talent acquisition and retention to the top of every

	Training	*e-learning*
1. Delivery	Push—Instructor Determines agenda	Pull—Student Determines agenda
2. Responsiveness	Anticipatory—Assumes to know the problem	Reactionary—Responds to problem at hand
3. Access	Linear—Has defined progression of knowledge	Non-linear—Allows direct access to knowledge in whatever sequence makes sense to the situation at hand
4. Timing	Synchronous—Teacher and student occupy the same time (sometimes the same place)	Asynchronous—Teacher and student can be separated by time and place
5. Symmetry	Asymmetric—training occurs as a separate activity	Symmetric—learning occurs as an integrated activity
6. Modality	Discrete—training takes place in dedicated chunks with defined starts and stops	Continuous—learning runs in parallel and never stops
7. Authority	Centralized—content is selected from a library of materials developed by the educators	Distributed—Content comes from the interaction of the participants as well as the educators
8. Personalization	Mass produced—Content must satisfy the needs of many	Personalized—Content is determined by the individual user's need to know in order to satisfy the needs of one.
9. Adaptivity	Static—Content and organization/taxonomy remains in their original authored form without regard to environmental changes	Dynamic—Content changes constantly through user input, experiences, new practices, business rules and heuristics.

Figure 6.1   Contrasting training with e-learning.

organization's list of critical success factors. The next logical step in mitigating the current circumstances is to maximize the utility of existing human capital. This involves educating the work force in a manner that tailors the methods and content to current needs while accurately anticipating future requirements.

Consider the volume of knowledge you have personally gained over the past year. How much was learned in a classroom or other formal training scenario?

As the individual worker becomes more valuable and more transitory, these problems only increase. Retention issues and internal reward systems are only part of the solution. In a free-agent economy, the onus will increasingly be on the employer to ensure the necessary tools are in place to remain competitive. Ideas, talent, products, and opportunities become lost or abandoned without proper infrastructure to deliver appropriately filtered knowledge to those who need it. A brilliant idea may occur in an instant, but mobilizing an uninitiated work force can take months or years.

The rapidity with which required skill sets change and time-to-market cycles shrink has begun to shift the notion of corporate education in the twenty-first century from the realm of classroom training to continuous education. Consider the volume of knowledge you have personally gained over the past year. How much was learned in a classroom or other formal training scenario? How about that of your sales force, engineering team, or marketing staff? Chances are the answer is "very little" in each case. This is not a new phenomenon, however the systems used to support on-the-job learning, such as apprenticeship and mentoring have been decimated by the discontinuity of today's workplace.

This realization has led to a new corporate imperative to align the dissemination of knowledge with the underlying corporate mission. The increased complexity of operations and opportunities obsoletes the traditional approach of prescriptive education where workers are expected to learn in advance the bulk of what is required to fulfill their jobs.

Yet simply relying on heuristics and random knowledge exchanges offers little means of keeping pace with a rapidly evolving skill requirements. In today's hypercompetitive market, the proverbial water cooler is an insufficient replacement for the formal classroom. The void left between formalized training and serendipitous discovery underscores the need for a just-in-time e-learning environment, where knowledge is dispensed as-needed rather than on a prescriptive basis.

The E-Learning Framework

Two fundamental benefits of e-learning are: the elimination of the barriers of time and distance, and the personalization of the user's experience.

E-learning removes the barriers of time and place and provides high levels of personalization to both the user and the task. By being integrated into the value-chain activity, e-learning delivers the most timely form of knowledge. By providing the tools by which a user can fully personalize the experience based on their skills and tasks e-learning creates a much more intimate and memorable learning experience (Figure 6.2).

Less than a quarter of over 1,000 organizations we surveyed on their e-learning practices indicated they had made exiting e-learning resource available to channel partners. Content and context can be used to provide a framework for understanding the various forms of learning, from generalized, Just-in-case classroom learning to Just-in-time, personalized e-learning.

Giving partners and customers the ability to be proactive rather than having to reactively respond to their needs for precise information creates greater immediacy for outside parties and less of a burden for the enterprise. This includes keeping indirect channel participants current on product capabilities; winning mind share of sales reps who push competing products (read "you sell what you know best"); promoting optimal utilization of products sold by indirect channels; and educating supply chain partners in the end use of products.

Given the growing demand for continuous learning within today's tight labor market, it is easy to associate e-learning solutions with limited focus on internal training initiatives. To do so at the expense of building business development and channel management is to miss

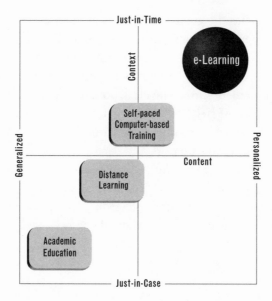

Figure 6.2   Content and context can be used to provide a framework for understanding the various forms of learning, from generalized, just-in-case classroom learning to just-in-time, personalized e-learning.

the real benefit of this new generation of technology. Internal training is typically linked to operational issues and cost control, not revenue generation. Unfortunately, many organizations already using e-learning practices are not fully leveraging its capabilities by limiting access to training, rather than revenue generating functions.

The Next Frontier: E-Learning Anytime, Anyplace, Any Device

As organizations grow more complex and increasingly mobile, the need to untether employees is leading to the pervasive incorporation of wireless devices in the e-learning framework. The added power and flexibility of cellular phones, pagers, and personal digital assistants offers developers new possibilities that take users beyond basic communications and administrative functions. Given the shift to single point access in today's corporate computing environment, e-learning will surely follow suit.

Where this has the greatest impact is in the use of e-learning as an integrated rather than as a separate discipline. The ability of e-learning solutions to be tightly integrated into a process rather than being yet one more process that competes for users' attention is key to its successful implementation. The classroom could be an executive conference room, an oil field, or a cramped coach airplane seat. E-learning needs to be able to dynamically alter both content and delivery to fit the student and the situation.

Wireless also increases the potential size of the audience for e-learning technologies by many orders of magnitude. Not only can a roving sales person or consultant access targeted, personalized content but front line employees who traditionally do not make personal computers part of their work environment can now realize the benefits of e-learning.

> The ability of e-learning solutions to be tightly integrated into a process rather than being yet one more process that competes for users attention is key to its successful implementation.

From harried sales executives trying to learn competitive intelligence during the cab ride to a client to a military equipment technician trying to repair a tank on the battlefield, the requirements of users can expand dramatically outside of the office environment. The need for e-learning for hazardous waste treatment personnel or emergency medical technicians takes on an entirely different meaning. Not only will content affect life-and-death situations, but such tools can cross the realm of learning media and enter into mission critical information delivery. The focus of the users must remain on the task at hand rather than the learning, raising again the importance of integrated e-learning as opposed to computer-based training.

With time-to-market pressures increasing, product lifecycles shortening, and human capital restrictions swelling, organizations are desperately searching for ways to expand bandwidth. As the economy becomes increasingly dependent on technology, the demand for skilled workers will consistently outstrip the supply. There will continue to be more good ideas than there are resources to execute business plans.

As organizations continue to be restricted by the number of competent individuals that can be mobilized, they will seek, in frustration, outside assistance to solve their knowledge and human capital woes. Using consultants, service providers, and freelancers only externalizes the problem. Third-party organizations experience the same talent shortage and infoglut that their customers do. All individuals in the extended enterprise must have access to customized learning content in a concise format.

As time is compressed in the Internet economy, the period allowed for conceptualizing and bringing ideas to fruition is attenuated. Effectively, this means that by using conventional training methods, computer-based or not, the time and money spent on training will become an increasingly larger component of development expenses and operational costs. Moreover, as long as the resulting bottleneck remains fixed due to use of archaic, just-in-case learning paradigms, training will increasingly become a more onerous hindrance to corporate growth.

By having a flexible, yet comprehensive e-learning infrastructure in place, organizations can maximize the utility of their most valuable resources—human capital and intellectual property. People, ideas, and opportunity are ephemeral. Using e-learning to capture and share ideas and market opportunities while they exist is critical to your company's success in the X-economy.

Trading on Time

To wrap up this chapter let's try to stretch the envelope just a bit beyond conventional wisdom. While e-learning emphasizes a point that we have made throughout this book, that success in the X-economy hinges on time, what if we go further down this path and actual frame time as an *exchangable* product?

Consider that in the X-economy there are two basic factors of success: time creation and time consumption. In effect, time becomes the greatest currency. And as with any other currency, as we have seen, it has liquidity.

Earlier in the book we talked about return on time as one measure of liquidity. Rather than measure how well an organization leverages its ability to produce a return on its investment of capital, return on time is a measure of how well an organization leverages its ability to generate a return on a given investment of time. If an organization can benchmark this ability, why could it not buy and sell it through an exchange?

In many ways *time* is the fundamental value proposition of an exchange. In the X-economy the greatest asset is not capital, intellect, or even innovation since each of these will reach some point of competitive parity as the tools and methods needed to achieve the five rules of the X-economy become widely available and understood. At that stage the currency of competitive advantage will be time.

But we do not mean this just in the sense of faster time to market or shorter business cycles. These are well-understood concepts. What we are referring to is something well beyond these—buy and sell time as a commodity.

As value chains continue to increase in their complexity and their interaction with each other two time-based phenomena will become apparent:

1. Increased chaos and unpredictability will create greater value of time as organizations attempt to coordinate an ever-increasing volume of opportunity with ever-decreasing duration of opportunity.
2. The ability to capture a market's interactions through Internet-based exchanges will allow time-navigation to become a fundamental aspect of the X-economy.

Chaos and the Value of Time

You may think that you are already in the business of time brokering. For example, if you pay a lawn service to cut your grass or if you bring your car in for an oil change rather than doing these jobs yourself (assuming you have the competency and tools to do the job), you have placed an implicit value on your time. Chances are that much of the impetus to have someone else do this is the increased chaos in your life and the need to focus on priorities—be they family, work, or just down time.

Organizations also place value on their resources by outsourcing certain tasks. The airline industry, similarly, places a value on time by charging you more for unpredictable travel than for predictable travel, which allows you to buy tickets well in advance of your trip (which is also why a more chaotic world results in greater revenue streams for businesses such as airlines). This is the same model that allows convenience stores to charge outrageous prices for goods that are readily available if you had only had the time to plan your purchases.

But in each of these cases the issue is more about the price of convenience than it is about the value of time.

A better example is the transportation logistics industry. It is estimated that 20 percent of all truck shipping capacity goes unused. To put it another way, 1 out of 5 of those enormous 18-wheel trucks you see traveling on the highways is empty. The reason? Logistics. It is nearly impossible to create a truck route that can meet the fast turnaround time required by buyers while using full capacity. Just-in-time shipping is becoming the norm for every industry creating an enormous waste of existing shipping resources. Traditional routes have been optimized using linear programming techniques that create a best possible route for suppliers and buyers. But as markets accelerate, these techniques cannot keep up with instantly changing demands.

Nistivo, an exchange focused on this particular problem has developed a business model that allows cross-industry suppliers to use this excess capacity by participating in a broader community. Nistivo is effectively brokering time and creating liquidity by bringing together buyers and sellers who would not otherwise know of each other's existence.

Furthermore, Nistivo creates recombinant liquidity by identifying new opportunities, across foreign industries and verticals, based on the demand chain. For instance, an automobile parts manufacturer may be shipping parts to the East Coast from Detroit with excess capacity. Nistivo will match the capacity with the need to ship computer chips in the same shipment as the truck passes through Cleveland.

It is a basic precept that although opportunities in the X-economy increase by orders of magnitude, the duration of any specific opportunity to match a time-based service with a time-based demand gets that much shorter. In this market space, market cycles are measured in intervals of minutes rather than months and years, and the value of matching the timing of supply and demand chains becomes the principal metric of competitive advantage.

The Time Traveler

It has been said that the Internet is the stream into which you never step twice. Constantly changing in unimaginably complex networks of connections and vast content, the ebb and flow of the Web is unlike anything we have experienced as a society.

But how do we record all of this enlightenment? The Web is to information what the moving picture was to photography. Rather than capturing a single instant in time, the Internet is capturing a virtually continuous stream of history, business, society, and every nuance of the global e-community we have formed.

Yet there is no way to trace this history. As the content and linkages of the Internet change, they are lost. We cannot roll back to a particular event, date, or time and view the millions of Web pages as they were at that moment and every subsequent moment to the present. We cannot even do this on the much smaller scale of a single Web site, or a collection of sites in a value chain. Or can we?

Until recently the answer was an unqualified no. This too changes in the X-economy. The ability to capture a historical view of one Web site, a collection of sites, or the entire World Wide Web will soon be possible.

At a social level, the implications are startling. Imagine being able to roll back the clock and get an absolutely precise historical record of everything from the weather and stock markets to the evolution of major sociopolitical trends. As the Web reflects an ever-increasingly complete view of the world, this becomes a time tunnel into the past.

The time portal will come to represent an important addition to the organization's tools for understanding its own activities, assets, and performance in an ongoing historical continuum.

Because the Internet technology underlying exchanges provides a means of continuously "recording" the content and activity that takes place in and through the portal, it can become the first reference point of a newly invigorated "corporate memory" function. While no doubt it will first be engaged as a tool for legal purposes (note the growing history of the role of e-mail in corporate and public litigation), it will also give tomorrow's managers a much more textured facility for understanding decisions and assets developed long before their time. As such it can become a vital tool for combating the negative effects of discontinuity at both the knowledge worker and the executive levels.

Exchanges that provide this sort of ability will have tremendous economic value, which is likely to be delivered through highly verticalized exchanges that focus on specific markets and demographics.

Takeaways

The final rule in this book dealt with the incredible shrinkage of time and the decrease over time of transaction intervals. In the technology arena, the oft-quoted Moore's law has shown us new processor product lifecycles and falling performance/prices, on a two-year pattern since the 1960s. And the Internet has given us the extreme example of the new realities of time competition: the concept of Internet Time. In this new economy, competitive time in Internet markets is effectively like "dog years," with several cycles taking place over the span of only a few calendar months. And this concept is not limited to technology alone.

While basic rules of commerce have remained essentially the same, the last decade has seen a dramatic change in the notion of lag time. Our ability to form connections faster has allowed organizations to disintegrate into much broader and more complex value chains. Exchanges have formed as a direct response to this situation and the resulting overnight disappearance of the latency in market interactions, has vanished in step with the accelerated pace of life. With little or no lag time in transactions, both buyers and sellers have become ever more conscious of time as the key metric of success.

We also discussed how ultimately supporting the new pace of the X-economy will require new methods of e-learning that enable just-in-time rather than just-in-case education.

While the time available to conduct business and form relation-ships seems to vanish, businesses are trying harder than ever to create intimacy with their customers and business partners. In an era where time is incredibly scarce, *time* actually becomes a tangible, ripe for brokering and trade. Companies are capitalizing on this notion through a number of novel approaches, but ultimately it may not be farfetched to "buy time" or be able to maximize its value using X-economy technologies.

Life After X

The historical task of our epoch consists in replacing, in disciplining the forces of production, compelling them to work together in harmony and obediently serve the needs of mankind. Only on this new social basis will man be able to stretch his weary limbs and—every man and every woman, not only a selected few—become a citizen with full power in the realm of thought.

But this is not yet the end of the road. No, it is only the beginning.

Leon Trotsky

We are 10 minutes into a 24-hour poker game.

Jim Champy

We started by saying that the X-economy was all about community.

It is one thing to benchmark this as a revolution based on how well it leverages the fundamental nature of humanity to build community. It is another thing all together to consider how the X-economy may change the fundamental nature of community itself.

How will the X-economy change our life, our work, our organizations, and our society? What might the resulting landscape of business resemble in 10 years time when exchanges have become a standard part of the economic landscape?

In ten year's time, you will not only be able to build your own personal exchange but we postulate that this exchange will be indistinguishable from you, your fortune, your livelihood, and your membership in a modern society.

What happens when we are brought face to face with unlimited amounts of information and computing power at the same time that the very notion of knowledge as an intangible is also being challenged? As with everything of value, accumulation of wealth and the basics of ownership will ultimately play a factor here.

Nearly 150 years ago, Karl Marx postulated that the economy is the fundamental force behind all human development. Eras change, wrote Marx in his manifesto, *Das Capital,* as the factors of production, (technology, resources, and organization) change. As wrong as Marx was about the mechanics of his grand plan, in this perception his work is widely accepted by today's economics profession.

What Marx did not understand, what he could not have understood, were the ultimate mechanics of community.

Could any economist, politician, revolutionary of any persuasion have been able to predict that community on a global scale would be something that came from within and not be imposed from without? Would any visionary have known that dis-integration of organizations and institutions would lead not to destructive disorder but rather constructive chaos? The answers are clear, but only in retrospect.

Marshal McCluhen's global village descended upon us overnight. We were infected by its virus while we were still trying to figure out where to itch. Global communications and instant connectivity have created opportunities and challenges few of us could have predicted. From the political collapse of the USSR to the economic rise of the European Union the world has changed in ways as profound as the results of either World War—with far less human toll.

The radical changes in today's era are not only transitioning the factors of production, from industrial to informational, but more importantly opening up new possibilities in the legal configurations which provide structure to the ownership of those factors of production at the most basic level of any community—the individual.

In ten years you will not only be able to build your own personal exchange but we postulate that this exchange will be indistinguishable from you, your fortune, your livelihood, and your membership in the modern society.

It is a shift that will turn the world on its head by delivering the means and the mechanism by which to deploy value to a spectrum of humanity broader than any political ideologist could have dreamt.

> We may well have the opportunity before us to move not only goods and services but indeed to move humanity itself forward a few steps in the process.

In more than 500 years of technological achievement, we have barely scratched the surface. Despite the overwhelming proliferation of communications technology the majority of the world lives in isolation. Seventy-five percent of humanity has yet to use a phone, Ninety-seven percent have yet to use the Internet, 99.5 percent have yet to use Napster.

We can rightfully say that that vast majority of humanity has better things to worry about, like shelter, food, and survival. But what of our original evolutionary triad: community, connectivity, commerce? If each does indeed act as a lever for the others, we may well have the opportunity before us to move not only goods and services but indeed to move humanity itself forward a few steps in the process.

The chart on page 222 reflects the number of years it took for each successive technology to reach a user population of 50 million. As the chart shows the time to 50 million users has been dropping precipitously even as the need for creating a new infrastructure has persisted. Cable television, for example, required laying hundreds of thousands of miles of cable along with the ramp-up of consumers to purchase set-top boxes. Yet when you add a third dimension to the chart by plotting each technology's penetration against worldwide growth in population (the middle set of bars), a daunting and nearly

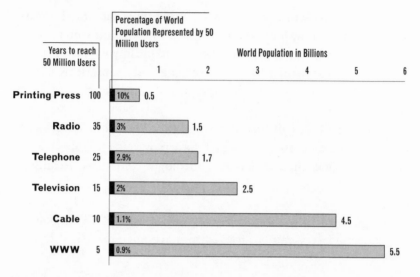

This chart dispels the familiar myth that is often used to make an argument for our increasing ability to deploy communication technology at ever faster rates. The bars plot the time elapsed for each of the technologies shown to reach 50 million users worldwide (dark band of each bar), the increasing worldwide population (gray bar), and the relative percentage of the worlds population represented by 50 million users. Clearly the time to 50 million users is a meaningless benchmark when worldwide population continues to explode at two net additions to the human race per second. The challenge is not simply broadcasting to much larger audiences but creating communities that can truly connect and communicate globally in the face of this explosion.

depressing dose of reality is provided—although the printing press took about 100 years to reach 10 percent of the world's population, it appears that none of these technologies have done much better to reach the same relative percentage of worldwide users! For example, consider that the telephone, which has been around for nearly 125 years, is still only used by one out of five people worldwide. Although we can debate the impact of broadcast as opposed to point-to-point communication a few percentage points either way, it is clear that the advances in our ability to deploy a technology platform for a global community are not as impressive as they may seem. There is, however, one possible exception—the World Wide Web. Tracking at nearly four times the pace of any other communication technology and already connecting 6 percent of the world's population, after only five years, the impact of connecting (not just broadcasting to) so many people so quickly is difficult to fathom.

Yet the obvious challenge is that we have to deal with the vastness of the impoverished ranks of humanity who cannot dream of affording a telephone or radio much less a device to connect to the internet. But this too is a matter of improving community. If the technologies on our chart share anything it is their ability to create new benchmarks for time to community. Each individual user of a telephone, radio, television, internet appliance or exchange has the potential to create a microcosm of commerce, incrementally increasing prosperity by increasing inclusion. There is little doubt that these technologies have helped to cast the net of inclusion farther into the ranks of humanity, from Gutenberg's bibles and Martin Luther's reformation leaflets to satellite driven education in remote villages.

Consider what that might mean for the X-economy. Simply put, the more dis-integrated our value chains become the more inclusive they become. It is not a solution for world hunger, but it may be a critical turning point in how we equitably measure the value and worth of the individual.

We have grown up in a world where the possession of things of matter was the greater measure of wealth and prosperity. We are fast transitioning into a world order where the possession of the intangible connections that form community are the principle construct of wealth. It is happening to makers of automobiles as surely as it is happening to each of us individually.

The radical changes in today's era are not only transitioning the factors of production, from industrial to informational, but, more importantly, opening up new possibilities in the communities that provide structure to the ownership of those factors of production.

Those who own these exchanges will surely be the most powerful forces, the kingpins, of tomorrow's economy. Then again, what if the exchanges were owned not by any one entity but rather by the communities themselves?

If you have any doubt, consider that the most lethal war in the next century, perhaps sooner, will be the one that embargos the international exchanges that provide food, fuel, and services to the world's nations and businesses.

Those who own these exchanges will surely be the most powerful forces, the kingpins, of tomorrow's economy. Then again, what if the exchanges were owned not by any one entity but rather by the communities themselves?

Speculating on the long-term impact that exchanges will have is clearly gazing into a crystal ball. We are as limited in our ability to appreciate the future impact of exchanges as the early users of prior technologies such as the airplane, telephone, and radio were in their own time. Perhaps more so given the speed with which changes occur in the ready communications infrastructure we now have.

It is not that we fail to understand the technology, but rather its implications on our social, economic, and political systems. It is a clear case of trying to prepare ourselves for those things that we don't know we don't know.

We have before us a Gordian knot of monumental proportions. It is the very nature of revolution to so disrupt the natural order of things as to obscure the view of the future.

However, we can speculate.

> The radical changes in today's era are not only transitioning the factors of production, from industrial to informational, but, more importantly, opening up new possibilities in the legal configurations which provide structure to the ownership of those factors of production.

Begin by asking yourself a simple question, "How far has humanity advanced in the last one thousand years?" Pick nearly any metric of productivity. For example, how many people can a single farmer feed, how much faster can we travel great distances, how much longer is our life expectancy. Amazingly, none of these answers offers an increase greater than a few orders of magnitude at best. There is, however, one notable exception, the speed with which we create community.

Whether it is Moore's law predicting the doubling of computer processing power every two years or Metcalf's law of the network's value being equal to the square of its nodes, the inescapable conclusion is that our ability to create connections today is barely a glimpse of what lies ahead.

Look again at our chart showing technology's adoption, specifically the last bar that shows the World Wide Web. Today the World Wide Web is accessed by some 400 million users. Yet the world's population has crested six billion. In other words, only 6.66 percent of humanity is connected to the Web. Consider that even the most popular Web sites attract only a small fraction of a percent of worldwide population. (for example, Napster with about 50 million users has a community of less than 1 percent of the world's population). In contrast, broadcast television routinely reaches a much larger audience of more than 200 million viewers at a time for broadcasts of global interest.

Yet, despite the fact that those affected represent a sliver of humanity, we talk about the radical nature by which the Internet and the X-economy has already altered our lives. Whose lives? Certainly not those of the other 93.6 percent of the world.

At the same time, we would claim that even within the shallow community of today's connected users, an equally small minority are using exchanges to form communities of trade. Perhaps 1 percent of the 400 million users, or 4 million participants worldwide represent the exchange savy. That's not quite seven one-hundreths of a single percent using what must be an equally insignificant percent of their available computing power to create communities with exchange technology that is barely embryonic.

This small group can make a possible one and one-half billion connections according to Metcalf's law. We know the practical reality is that a very small number of these connections will *actually* be made, but at least we have a benchmark to start with.

What might it mean if we were able to increase the raw availability and access to community over the next decade by changing this equation by even a slight margin.

If we continue to assume that only 10 percent of the people who are connected to and can participate in an exchange will participate, then raising the number who can participate to 2 percent of the worldwide population increases the potential connection to nearly one and one-half trillion.

> The greatest possession in the coming century will be the community and the connections we form within it.

If the number of actual participants increased to 50 percent of possible participants then at 5 percent of the world's population the result would be 225 trillion connections. That is five orders of magnitude higher and more than 140,000 times greater than the number of community connections that are available online in today's world. Yet we are still including less than 5 percent of the world's population!

The numbers are staggering. By way of contrast, the number of calculations per second has increased by four orders of magnitude in the final decade of the twentieth century.

And all of this still factors in the assumption that possible connections would be only 10 percent of what they could be based on using just 10 percent of available computing power.

In this world, exchanges will be as prevalent as telephones are today. They will be built and owned not just by multinational corporations but by an intricate food chain stretching all the way down to the individual. And it is here that they will ultimately have their greatest impact.

Perhaps the greatest possession in the coming century will be the community and the connections we form within it.

We made it clear at the beginning of this book that X represented the extremities of markets and the economy to which power has been slowly but surely shifting for centuries. We said that every social, political, and economic system is being further decentralized into entities that are apparently uncontrolled by centralized authorities and instead ruled by their communities. So why not go the next step now, and envision what it might look like to move that power further into the hands of the people who make up those communities.

Why limit the idea of the exchange to large enterprise or global value chains? For that matter, why limit it to business, large or small, as we know it today? Exchanges, whether called portals or online communities, are already being used by individuals to build instant communities that serve their economic and personal interests. From striking pilots to people with disabilities to the mass of free agents seeking job placements, exchanges are serving to democratize access to community.

Think of it. Whether you are creating a business or a political party, the greatest impediment has always been the time it takes to create the community. When this changes, how might the world change?

What will it look like, this brave new X-world, this global community?

Let's keep it simple and personal. Imagine the scenario, a dimly lit lawyer's office with solemn faces staring blankly across a dark mahogany conference table.

A son and daughter gathered to hear the reading of their beloved father's last will and testament.

The lawyer begins to read. His low monotone droning on for what seems to be hours until he pauses and readies himself.

". . . to my beloved son, I leave my entire estate, cash, equities, real estate, and personal property . . ."

A solemn daughter looks down as her heart drops.
The lawyer continues,

". . . except for the exchange that I used to build my expansive fortune. This I leave to my daughter, who I trust will use it to build a better world."

What do you think, an even split between siblings? Far fetched? What great change hasn't been? It's only as unlikely as the degree to which you discount the ability of commerce to evolve, to reinvent itself in dramatic new ways from within; beyond the need for external constraints and interventions, toward an economy of community—an X-economy.

INDEX